Business Writing at Its Best

Business Writing at Its Best

Minerva Neiditz
Institute of Writing
University of Connecticut

McGraw-Hill
New York   San Francisco   Washington, D.C.   Auckland   Bogotá
Caracas   Lisbon   London   Madrid   Mexico City   Milan
Montreal   New Delhi   San Juan   Singapore
Sydney   Tokyo   Toronto

McGraw-Hill

A Division of The McGraw·Hill Companies

Library of Congress Cataloging-in-Publication Data

Neiditz, Minerva Heller, 1932–
    Business writing at its best / Minerva H. Neiditz.
      p. cm.
    Includes bibliographical references.
    ISBN 0-7863-0137-6
    1. Business writing.   2. English language—Business English.
  I. Title
  HF5718.3.N45 1994
  808'.06665—dc20   93–23668

Printed in the United States of America
     5 6 7 8 9 0 DOC 1 0 9 8

P R E F A C E

In the systems age, we tend to look at things as parts of larger wholes. A problem is not solved by taking it apart, but by viewing it as part of a larger problem.

Russ Achoff

There are a number of college textbooks on the market that address technical writing, business writing, argument, visual design, persuasion, critical thinking, etc. Many of these texts are excellent. But there is no brief text that covers all these topics and provides real-world writing samples to illustrate how to change mediocre writing into excellent writing. Nor do they provide exercises that reinforce the learning of necessary principles. This text has been tested on over 15,000 clients and students. It has proven its usefulness, both in teaching a myriad of stylistic principles, and in helping people:

- change the way they think
- structure their thoughts before they begin to write
- see ideas quickly because of visual design
- find original ideas and fresh language
- communicate knowledge to a variety of audiences, including cross-cultural audiences.

You may well wonder why I've grouped all this material together. A better question would be: Can it be done? Can one learn enough about style, logic, visual structure, persuasion, creative thinking and cross-cultural communication in less than 300 pages to make the struggle worthwhile? The answer is "yes." Try it; you'll see.

May I remind you that *The Elements of Style* by Strunk and White contains only 85 small pages. David Lambuth's *Golden Book on Writing* is only 79 pages. The quality of these brief books has withstood the test of time.

But brevity is only one consideration. I am hoping you will see instantaneously how mediocre writing can become excellent writing. The "before and after" samples are meant to be *gestalts*, images of the whole which convey meaning through visual structure. Meaning leaps off the page in the "after" samples and reaches the mind's eye. Sentences are only the flesh on the skeleton. But it is the skeletal structure that transmits meaning to the right brain. Your eye will pick up immediately the purpose of the document and what must be done about it.

The advantage in learning visual techniques is to save the busy reader time and to prevent misunderstanding. Obviously the right words and logical organization matter. But I cannot stress enough how important it is to make your information or argument **visible**.

In addition, there is much talk today about transformative ways of managing people in the new, global economy. Rationality and creativity were always thought of as contrasting characteristics and, in large corporations, rationality is usually rewarded: facts, nothing but the facts. But the faster things change, the less you can use facts and the more you need imagination. That is why I have included a chapter on creative thinking.

Writing **is** thinking. We often assume that means critical, sequential, logical thinking. Much of the time it does. Indeed, you will learn my version of Toulmin logic because it is a method which works in the business world. In addition, Edward De Bono's lateral thinking is an imaginative approach which solves problems that cannot be resolved through logic alone. I skim the surface in a brief introduction of ways to loosen up the mind, but you can always refer to the bibliography for references to this fruitful field. Often my clients have found this part of the course the most enjoyable.

Last, I feel it is important to deal with issues of intercultural communication. If you wish, you can think of the chapter on international communication in regard to a multi-cultural workplace. There is no substitute for knowing differences in tone, customs, courtesy and strategy for individuals from many cultural backgrounds.

So now you have my rationale for grouping these topics together. As for the order in which they appear, I've started with the easier ones first and built toward the more difficult ones later. This is in keeping with a good exercise regimen: you must warm up by stretching before tackling a more challenging workout, either physical or mental.

I would like to thank my assistant, Lane Barrow, for his patience, intelligence and cheerful irreverence as well as his many suggestions on this project. He edited and typed, read and reread, added and removed, until the book attained its present form. I couldn't have done it without him. I would also like to thank the following people who helped me revise the book: Jean Keith Bennett, Betsy McKay, Michael Feldman, Susanne Clair, Robert Kyff, Charlene Schultz, my students at the University of Connecticut, particularly the Executive MBA class of 1994, and Lou Loomis of the Hartford Critical and Creative Thinking Institute.

Contents

PRINCIPLES OF CRITICAL AND CREATIVE THOUGHT

PRINCIPLES OF 1994 AND BEYOND

CONCLUSION

Models/Formats

I N T R O D U C T I O N

Man is an animal that lives in language as a fish lives in water.
Robert Scholes

Do you avoid writing? Whether it's a long report or a short letter, do you stare at the page, bite your pencil, go to the refrigerator, think of watering the plants? Have you developed writing anxiety? Do you feel trepidation each time a piece of writing is due?

If you've answered yes to any of these questions, this text will help. But the text is not just for people who avoid writing. It will also appeal to those who have a vested interest in writing well. This includes managers and executives, intellectual explorers, teachers of writing and professionals of all kinds (engineers, lawyers, social workers, scientists, grant writers, public relations specialists, economists, financial analysts, accountants, etc.).

Your writing will improve as your feelings of self-confidence increase. That feeling comes when you know and use certain basic principles. However, these principles are meant to be guidelines, not algorithms.

In this text, you'll be moving from basic principles to exercises that embody those principles. The portfolio of writing that you'll create will show that you've achieved a higher level of communication, that you're in control of the messages you send, that those messages are received and that your readers will respond with the results you want.

What will you gain?

- **First**, you'll gain a feeling of self-confidence and an end to anxiety.
- **Second**, you'll find that you'll be in demand. Excellent writing correlates highly with the ability to *think* well, analyze, make decisions and persuade.
- **Third**, you'll be in command of the many forms that writing takes in the business world. You will bridge the gap between academic writing and the clear, concise, organized and persuasive writing required by employers.
- And **last**, you'll be able to do the best job you can do, which inevitably leads to a sense of fulfillment and pride.

P R I N C I P L E S   O F

STYLE

1

Write for Your Readers, Not for Yourself

The essential question is: Who's talking to whom?

Before you begin to write, you should ask yourself three questions:

- To whom am I writing?
- What purpose will this communication serve?
- Is that purpose clear to my reader?

At work, you will probably write to inform or to persuade or a combination of both. The information has to be clearly presented because the decision-maker needs it to do his or her job. This is not the kind of writing you've written for professors who want to see how you arrived at your conclusions or how gracefully you express your ideas. Few people in the business world are interested in the process of your discovery. Everyone is pressed for time.

At work, you tell people what *they* need to know *in the order that is most useful to them*. Therefore, you must first determine who your readers will be and then arrange the information or the argument in an order that reveals your understanding of the readers' needs. You can't control all reader responses, but you can make some reasonable predictions about how readers will react to what you write.

3

In the following "before" example about a teleconference with Patchwork Airlines, the writer is addressing his teammates concerning additional work that the team feels would be a waste of time. These people have been under pressure to maintain both the quality and quantity of their output. As one worker said, "Rising demands, combined with painful layoffs have left us emotionally and physically drained."

Before

From: Regional Manager, Asia Pacific Division
About: Teleconference with Patchwork Airlines

Patchwork Airlines has requested the resumption of regular technical discussions between Hub Industries and their Technical Services Department. The discussions will take the form of a series of evening teleconferences. The discussions will be led by Marvin King, Manager Technical Services at Patchwork. His office has provided an agenda, which is attached to this memo.

I have evaluated the list of items from Patchwork, and assigned responsibility to those organizations which seem best able to provide appropriate response. The first teleconference will be on Tuesday, Dec. 1 at 9:00PM. I would like to request that each responsible organization provide its response to the agenda by November 30th.

I will lead the discussion from the Hub Industries side. Responsible personnel from any organization are welcome to present the results of their agenda items during the teleconference. Please coordinate your participation with my office.

The writer of this memo confessed: "Originally, I thought I was conveying simple information. When I rethought the memo and the principle of writing for the reader, I realized I needed to inspire action in the face of negative experience. My first memo was stale. It completely ignored the dread that my team felt regarding the resumption of the teleconferences. My rewrite adds lightness and empathy and a reward. The tone is conversational and motivational."

After

> **From:** Regional Manager, Asia Pacific Division
> **About:** Pizza with Patchwork Airlines
>
> Our friends at Patchwork Airlines have done it again! Just when we thought it was safe to go home at night, Marvin has asked us to resume our weekly evening teleconferences. I know what a burden this has been to everyone, as we have all given up a great deal of our personal time during the last round of meetings. Therefore, in order to minimize the impact of the next round of meetings, I have arranged a short and focused agenda (see attached).
>
> The first teleconference will be on Tuesday, Dec. 1 at 9:00PM. I would like to encourage everyone to develop a preliminary response by Monday, November 30, for review. I will lead the discussion from our side, as we all work hard to strengthen our relationship with this important customer. Your personal participation in the evening teleconference is a valuable contribution and is highly encouraged. Just remember — the pizza is on me.
>
> Thanks for your help.

If the primary reader is the vice president you report to, you might not have to give him background on the topic. But if the report or memo is going both to the V.P. and to the president, that background might be necessary. What do you do? If you're presenting an argument, put that argument on the first page and place the background information last.

The following "before" sample is an example of writing aimed at the top executive of an insurance company. It looks organized, but it does not meet the needs of the reader, who wants a brief, clear argument for or against a new computer system.

What the CEO needs is the complete argument with the reasons supporting the proposal and costs — then the recommendation of a vendor. The first presentation skips about, scattering the necessary supporting evidence under "miscellaneous." The "after" sample is respectful of the reader's time and energy, showing a thoughtful format that groups information logically.

Look at the topic headings, and the order in which they flow. That will give you the skeleton. Start with the "skull," the *ideas* that the brain has to take in. Then go to the arms, legs, feet, etc.

Before

PROPOSAL
To purchase for $550,000 a PDP-11 computer system for typesetting, inventory control, and department operating systems from Composition Systems, Inc.

INTRODUCTION
The primary reason for acquisition is upgrade of the typesetting system. The present PDP-8 system is 5 years old, technologically obsolete, and cannot interface with other text-processing systems.

The capability of the proposed system presents the opportunity to accomplish two additional needs: (1) Upgrade the Supply Inventory System, which will be at capacity by June 1988, and (2) Provide department systems for operations management. We will phase out the IBM 1401 Tab Card System presently in use within three years.

INTERFACE
The proposed system is totally interactive and capable of processing multiple tasks concurrently. In addition to work keyed by printing personnel, the system will accept work generated in systems in the line of business areas by on-line video terminals, magnetic or paper tape.

MISCELLANEOUS
Our present system is at capacity, due to input limitations and slow typesetter processing. Inability to interface with other system requires all input to be rekeyed by printing personnel or outside vendors.

The volumes shown represent significant increases that can only be accepted in an upgraded system. Volumes provided by lines of business were expressed by numbers of books or book pages, and converted to dollars to combine with printing volume.

The processed system is a major step up that will provide capacity beyond the five-year volume projections. The comparison of typesetters illustrates the point.

Present Photon Pacesetter   50 newspaper lines/minute
Proposed: Metro/Set   1,000 newspaper lines/minute

The volumes from the lines are predominantly Book pages of fairly uniform format. We can easily maintain records of actual vs. estimated volumes to audit performance against this proposal.

Capital Cost $550,000
> Includes computer hardware for typesetting, inventory control, and department systems; software for typesetting and general systems control; installation; training; logo scanner and stabilization processor. Does not include software for inventory control ($10-20,000) or operating systems ($20-$40,000).

INCREMENTAL DIRECT OPERATING COSTS
> Maintenance & Operating Supplies $75,798

TIMING
> Delivery of hardware is estimated to be 12 months from date of purchase order.

IMPLEMENTATION PLAN
> To be prepared on approval of purchase. Joe Fragione will be the Systems Manager and will receive training prior to equipment installation.

After

PROPOSAL
To purchase a PDP-11 computer system for typesetting, inventory control, and department operating systems.

WHY WE NEED A NEW SYSTEM

1. To handle projected workloads
The present system, a five-year-old PDP-8, is working at capacity. Projections show that our need will outrun its capacity by 6% in 1988, 10% in 1989, 16% in 1990, 25% in 1991, and 31% in 1992.

The new PDP-11 will handle even more work than the projections forecast as a comparison of the typesetters indicates:

    Present: 50 newspaper lines a minute
    Proposed: 1,000 newspaper lines a minute

2. To interface with other text-processing systems
While the PDP-8 cannot interface, the PDP-11 will accept not only work keyed by printing personnel but also work from on-line video terminals and magnetic paper tape.

3. To upgrade the Supply Inventory System
The PDP-11 can enlarge this system, which will otherwise be at capacity by June 1988.

4. To provide department systems for operational management
We will phase out the IBM 1401 Tab Card System within three years. The PDP-11 can take over and extend our capacity for operations management.

5. To meet the needs of new markets
For example, A&PR could have on-line terminals for publication input; the GIO Communications Plus Unit could process its benefits statements; and the stereo area could use the high-speed keying.

In fact, any user could manipulate text, convert it into graphics and otherwise control the creation and alteration of its data. The "Office of the Future" requires interactive systems.

COSTS: We have studied three ways to meet our needs – updating the PDP-8, leasing a PDP-11, or buying one. In October 1986, we proposed spending $312,000 to update the PDP-8. While that cost is low, the development of the PDP-11 has now made such an upgrade unwise because:

- the PDP-8 cannot handle the projected work.
- the PDP-8 is not compatible with the GIO's PDP-11.
- the proposal assumed the PDP-8 inventory system would be upgraded separately.
- the proposal did not provide for the PDP-8's taking over the IBM 1401 systems for department management and cost-accounting.

1. **Capital Cost: $550,000:** This includes computer hardware for typesetting, inventory control, and department systems; software for typesetting and general systems control; installation; training; and typesetter with logoscanner and stabilization processor.

2. **Software for inventory control: $10,000 to $20,000**
3. **Software for department systems: $20,000 to $40,000**
4. **Depreciation: $59,400 per year**
5. **Incremental direct operating costs: $75,798**

The improvements seem obvious after you see the rewritten document. But such clarity is difficult to achieve because most writers write for themselves, not for their readers. They do not take the time to do a thorough audience analysis.

The following seven questions should help you think through the problem of **audience**:

1. Who is your audience? Is it multiple?

2. How much does that audience know about your message(s)?

3. How do you think your readers will respond? What attitudes will they have? Receptive? Hostile? Indifferent?

4. How do you *want* them to respond?

5. What objections will they have? What questions?

6. Have you omitted any significant information, concepts or context?

7. Is communication in harmony with the policies of your company?

Depending on the purposes of your communication, you will have to answer many of these questions before you begin or complete your document.

The next example is a **bad** memo because it defies the reader totally. We know that the audience is division heads, but we can't see quickly the purpose, the background, the questions that are being answered or the action that will be taken. The "after," with three topic headings, is one possible solution to this unnecessarily obscure, obtuse way of communicating.

Before

To: Division Heads
From: Joe Manager
Date: May 29, 1993
About: Progress Report

As you may recall, customer focus sessions were conducted in June and July, for the purpose of understanding what our customers value or would value in the products and services offered. The overall objective of this initiative is to improve the quality of services and products.

The documentation from the sessions was completed and verified by the participants early in September. The past few weeks have been spent re-categorizing the customer value statements into processes. The next step involves applying TQM (Total Quality Management) tools and methodologies acquired through formal training, to address the high priority issues identified in the focus sessions.

In order to stay in touch with our systems, representatives from various divisions have joined the quality design team. This is just one way in which we hope to enlist participation from you, our customers.

The design team is responsible for generating ideas for process improvements and making recommendations specific to the high priority value statements. The recommendations will first be presented to internal management for review, followed by presentation to two customer review committees. The purpose of these review committees is to solicit feedback regarding the proposed solutions.

The two review committees will represent different levels of customers. The first level review committee will contain one focus session participant from each of the nine focus sessions. The second level review committee will contain one management-level representative from each division. This management-level representative will be responsible for communicating the design teams' recommendations to their divisions and providing feedback to the design team.

Over the next few weeks, I will be contacting you in an attempt to clarify the objectives of this project if necessary, and to identify the representatives for the two customer committees. If you have any questions in the meantime, please do not hesitate to call.

After

To:　Division Heads
From:　Joe Manager
Date:　May 29, 1993
About:　Progress Report on Customer Feedback Project

I am updating you on the progress of the Customer Feedback Project.

Background

Customer focus sessions were conducted in June and July. The participants completed surveys aimed at determining what our customers value or would value in the products and services we offer. The survey results have been reviewed and re-categorized for easier analysis. The next step involves applying TQM (Total Quality Management) tools and methodologies to address the high priority issues identified in the focus sessions.

Current Developments/Recommendations

I am pleased to report that representatives from some divisions have joined the quality design team. As you know, the design team is to take the lead in responding to the issues raised in the customer focus sessions.

I propose that the recommendations be presented to internal management first, and then to two customer review committees. I believe two review committees are necessary to better represent different levels of customers. The first level review committee will be made up of nine focus session participants. The second level review committee will contain one management-level representative from each division, who will be the communications liaison between the design teams and his/her division.

Planned Action

I will contact you in the next two weeks to identify the representatives of the two customer committees. Please contact me if you have any questions.

Now let's take a look at a few *good* examples that take the audience into account. These examples communicate information easily and persuade the reader to do what the writer proposes.

Good Example

A DESCRIPTION OF STAFFING NEEDS

From: C.A. Champion, Project Manager
To: Aetna Project D Team
Date: November 28
Subject: Staffing Needs as a Result of Decreasing Claim Count

The Claim Department is working on a project concerning the Field Claim Staffing needs as a result of a decreasing claim count. This project originated in the June Progress Review Meeting. Using the Project D team will give a more accurate review of our regions for this project.

The project will consider the following components:

1. Review new claim count & staffing trends by <u>Claim Product Line</u>.

    Plan: Determine, by each regional Office, trends in Property, Liability and Workers' Compensation Lines.

2. Analyze particular claim offices and recommend, as appropriate, consolidation of functions, duties, or offices under <u>current</u> staffing guidelines.

    Plan: Isolate selected offices (those with larger staff counts) that seem to afford the greatest opportunity for savings:

    - Recommend consolidations, as appropriate.

3. Review <u>current</u> staffing guidelines.

    Plan: Review current workload guidelines and consider:

    - Shift of business from Personal to Commercial lines
    - Accumulation impact of new programs, reinspection, self-inspection, Fair Claim Practice Acts
    - Impact of EEO
    - Change in personnel or level of knowledge
    - Loss or gain of Reclaim or Processing function
    - Any other duties gained or lost
    - Position of Telephone Adjustment Process.

Good Example

A REQUEST FOR GUIDELINES

From: John Jones, Insurance Claims Dept.
To: Randy Miles, Legal Assistant
Subject: Guidelines for School Risk Asbestos Exposure

Background: Millions of tons of asbestos have been used in the construction of schools, factories, hospitals, etc., in the past. This use is causing asbestosis, mesothelioma and bronchiogenic carcinoma. Discovery from first exposure to first manifestation of the ailment can be as long as 50 years.

Consequently, the issue of coverage is complex. Attached is a file of the current status of litigation disputes.

Problem: How do we proceed with school risks under our CMP Institutional Program?

Solution: It is essential that you write some specific guidelines on new and renewal business to avoid individual or class action suits.

Further Comments: Take into consideration that the majority of these accounts are of new construction and that it's hard to know how much asbestos was used. Also consider the media publicity.

Good Example

A REVIEW OF A PROCESS

From: Ralph Marsden, Director of Marketing
To: All Marketing Representatives
Subject: Special Bid Process

Many of you are aware that we have implemented a new pricing strategy, but you may not be familiar with the new pricing process that goes along with it. To eliminate confusion and speed the process for obtaining high-end pricing, here's a quick review of the process.

- Fill out Pricing Request Form
- Meet with me to review the decision criteria
- I will return a specific price to you within 48 hours

Some hints to ensure that everything goes smoothly:

- Run the detailed configurations (including memory and channels)
- Be prepared to explain the details of the customer's last transaction
- Be aware of response time requirements

The purpose is to provide the best solution at the right price to every customer, the first time. Please call me if you have any questions or would like to discuss the process further.

EXERCISE **1** **Let's look at another "before" example. The purpose is to request more staff. Could this purpose be made clearer? How? Can you think of other ways to improve the original by asking the questions your readers might ask? Analyze the audience(s). What objections might they have? What questions? Now rewrite this memo.**

This office has not had the luxury of full staffing at any time in recent history. There is no relief from unceasing pressure due to limitation of staff, even during this period of low employment.

A comparison of February/January non-monetary time lapse and first-payment time lapse provides a clear indication of the inflexible position of the office to meet holiday time off and influxes of work such as employer appeals and monthly deluge of referee decisions.

A request for additional help can be made in any classification since we are marginally staffed in supervisory personnel, fact finding, claims examiners, and clerical positions. In each category we can set aside <u>no</u> <u>time</u> for training, much less tolerate absenteeism of any nature, or sudden influx of work.

A possible solution would be to share a technician, a fact finder, a claims examiner, and a typist for 2 – 3 days per week with another unit. To avoid friction, this arrangement would have to be placed on a predetermined schedule. However, as previously reported, help from another unit must not be assigned on the basis of expendability due to inadequacy or marginal competence. This selection results in a deterioration rather than an enhancement of performance of this office.

Examples of potential assistance:

a. To relieve supervisors: A technician – 2 days weekly to complete records and reports that are the tools used for constant monitoring and evaluation.

b. To relieve fact finders: An additional fact finder – to reduce the impact on flow of work that occurs if time is diverted due to non-postponable training, lost due to absenteeism or absorbed due to sudden influxes such as employer appeals and surge of referee decisions.

c. To relieve claims examiners: Basically same solution as (b) above.

d. To relieve the clerical section: Same as (b) above.

2

PRINCIPLE

"Speak" Your Writing to Your Audience with Control

Clear writing is just talk put into ink.

Jonathan Price

Speak your writing. That's both easy and difficult to do. It's easy because we usually speak fluently to an individual. It's difficult because we often have multiple audiences when we write and sometimes we don't even know to whom our proposal or report will go. However, what is absolutely true is that **people**, not machines, will read our work. Therefore, we shouldn't sound like machines. A spoken voice is easier to understand than the voice of a robot.

There is, of course, a difference between speaking **to** and speaking **with** an audience. You shouldn't sound like someone on a podium. You don't want to be condescending. Nor do you usually want to intimidate, although there are occasions on which you might **want** to sound like a lawyer. *The best kind of business writing is an equal speaking with an equal.*

Not a commander ordering troops into battle (Francis, **meet** me tomorrow at 2:00!).

Not a father or mother talking down to a child (Francis, you've **got** to meet me tomorrow at 2:00 or you'll miss your doctor's appointment).

Not a **close** friend (Oh Francis, I'd **love** to meet you tomorrow at 2).

Not a potential client pushing away a salesman (Oh, yes...uh... Francis...please call me next week).

But an equal speaking to an equal in a respectful tone (Francis, can you meet me tomorrow at 2?).

When we speak, we usually make all those adjustments automatically, drawing people toward us, pushing them away, talking down to, talking up to. That's the music that conveys our true message. Obviously, that music changes, depending on our relationship to the reader, the situation or context, our purpose, our subject, our personality and the reader's personality. But somehow all of that comes together automatically when we speak.

EXERCISE **2** **Let's look at some sentences to see if they follow this principle. Consider the context and the tone. Could you speak these sentences?**

1. Please be advised in the above-captioned memo that your employment will be terminated on 6 May, 1990. (*Context*: Memo to an employee who has worked for the company for 5 years. Tone? Effectiveness?)

2. Employees working on operations where liquid coolant is used should be instructed to wear hand protection and to practice personal hygiene in regard to the washing of hands and arms that might come in contact with the liquid or spray from the operation. (*Context*: Excerpt from company guidelines. Tone? Effectiveness?)

3. There will occasionally be special circumstances that may call for frequent revision of the forms, but we believe that most documents once approved will only require minor annual adjustments and could remain in effect for varying lengths of time (up to four years) after which period they would have to be rewritten and the program strategy would have to be approved. (*Context*: Government document. Can you speak this?)

4. I have taken much longer than I intended to in sending you this promised letter to follow up on the conversation about the interest

there might be in examining the possibility of undertaking a new research project. (*Context*: Letter to a client. Can this be improved?)

5. After corresponding with Mrs. Hudson, I am herewith returning your check for deposit to Mrs. Hudson's account with the proviso that this explanation which follows will suffice. I await your response. (Would you speak this way?)

6. It has come to my attention that it was requested in previous correspondence that a change be made with regard to your mailing address. It is also my understanding that your advisor has been notified and has become involved and feels that there is some concern with the fact that non-delivery occurred. I can assure you that we are doing what we can to rectify this matter. (*Context*: Letter to a client. How could this be improved?)

7. In response to your inquiry concerning…
   Per your request…
   Please feel free to call me…
   (Would you speak these openings?)

8. As mentioned in our previous correspondence, the open balance on your account has become delinquent. Payment must be received soon to keep your account in good standing. Please contact our Accounting Office if there is a question about your billing. Your prompt attention to this matter will insure continued credit privileges with our firm. (*Context*: Overdue notice after 12 months. Tone?)

3

P R I N C I P L E

Trust Your Ear as You Listen to Your Voice on the Page

A bore is a person who talks when you wish him to listen.

Ambrose Bierce

As you change your writing to reflect the natural patterns of human speech, you'll find that you will automatically take into account how you want to sound to your particular readers. You might **want** to sound formal. That's fine. Formal writing is appropriate for formal reports. But being *formal* is **not** necessarily being *pompous*, *wordy*, or *abstract*, the cardinal sins. Equally important is remembering that good communications involves three people: (1) you as writer, (2) you as listener, (3) your reader "listening" to what you have written.

EXERCISE **3**

Speak these sentences out loud. Listen how they sound to your ear. Put a *check* next to the sentences that sound okay. If a sentence doesn't sound okay, put an 'X' next to it. Try to identify the audience each sentence is directed to.

1. I sent the letter to him.
   I sent him the letter.

2. We cannot deliver the material.
   We can't deliver the material.

3. That is something in which the CEO is interested.
   That is something the CEO's interested in.
   That's something the CEO's interested in.
   The CEO is interested in that product.

4. What is wrong with this study? It has two flaws.
   What is the error in the communication we have received?
   There are, in connection therewith, two deficiencies.
   This study has two flaws.

5. That report led to a series of recommendations of which many have since been implemented.

6. The contractor contended that the test cases contained unacceptable error rates, impacting upon the contractor's ability to start their integrated testing of the system.

7. Distributed herewith is a survey of some 24 U.S. agribusiness firms with experience and/or interest in S.E. Asian business opportunities.

4

P R I N C I P L E

Be Clear and Brief

Everything that can be thought at all can be thought clearly.
Everything that can be said can be said clearly.

Ludwig Wittgenstein

Just as there are sins in writing, there are virtues: clarity and brevity are among the highest. I believe that it's good to write clearly, that anyone can, and that clarity often requires brevity. Therefore, how can you untangle knotted sentences, gobbledygook, bureaucratese, legalese, and other forms of poor writing?

It's simple. You sweat it out in your second draft. You edit. Or better yet, you learn to write simply and clearly in your first draft. Depending on the length and complexity of the piece, you will probably have to edit several drafts.

In the sample on the next page, a government employee shows how she color codes her editing, using a red pencil for the first go-round and a green pencil for the second. Here's an example of her work at the Bureau of the Census (the plain text shows her first draft in red pencil, the **bold** shows her changes in green pencil):

for us
We would like to emphasize how important it is ↑ to receive the necessary documentation
of the legal requirements for the data to support the inclusion of specific questions on the
↑ ~~for the questionnaire content and your comments on our Plan for the Participation of the~~
1990 questionnaire for Puerto Rico.   *soon*
~~Government of Puerto Rico in the Promotion for the 1990 Census~~ ↑ ~~in the near future.~~
Enclosed is   *receiving*
~~Attached you will find~~ the schedule ~~we must comply with~~ for ~~receipt of~~ comments
    submitting them to the Office of Management and Budget
and ↑ ~~submissions to OMB~~ for clearance **of the Puerto Rico questionnaire.**

You can create your own system. For example, first edit your work for **deadwood**, words that convey no meaning. Pay attention to transitional words and the "flow" of language as well as the tone. And, of course, begin writing in a voice you would use to speak to your audience.

You will find in many texts on writing an overreaction to the Gunning Fog Index (see Appendix 1) and similar readability formulae. Some feel that these tools have been overworked, that you cannot achieve clarity and brevity by just using short words and short sentences. A brief sentence like "Ontogeny recapitulates phylogeny" is not necessarily clear. All of this is true.

However, I have found in my practice as a writing consultant that <u>many</u> people write sentences like the ones below. And the simple guideline of keeping a sentence to three lines and avoiding wordiness and polysyllabic abstractions works wonders. *Most writing can lose a third to half of its bulk as the following examples show.* I have annotated the "befores" with the numbers of the Principles that have been violated.

Before

I am enclosing <u>herewith</u> *(violates #5)* a copy of the guidelines recently <u>adopted by the Examination Council</u> *(violates #9)* for determining whether to assess civil money penalties. The <u>factors identified by the Examination Council are those factors</u> *(violates #4 and #5)* that we use before the Enforcement Review Committee to determine whether to proceed with a civil money penalty. I request that you be aware of these factors and <u>take them into consideration when you are evaluating whether to recommend</u> *(violates #8)* a civil money penalty action.

(78 words)

After

The Examination Council has recently adopted the enclosed guidelines, which identify the factors we use before the Enforcement Council in determining whether to assess civil money penalties. Please be aware of these factors when you consider recommending such penalties.

(39 words)

Before

<u>It is especially important that</u> *(violates #10)* concentration <u>be placed</u> *(violates #9)* on those employees in the <u>four-through-seven-year experience level</u> *(violates #4)*. This is usually the critical period when an individual makes his or her decision on their career with OCC. This study <u>looks at</u> *(violates #8)* the dollar costs in permitting mid-level employees to attend regional staff conferences accompanied by their spouses. For the purpose of this study, I have assumed that grade levels 9 through 12 correspond to experience levels of four through seven years.

(83 words)

After

This study estimates the dollar cost of inviting the spouses of grade 9 through 12 employees to attend regional staff conferences. These grades are especially important, since it is at this level that employees decide whether to stay with OCC.

(40 words)

Throughout this text, we will look at many "before and after" examples. I believe that such models show in vivid detail the value of **rewriting**. Study these models carefully. Note the improvements and how they were attained. Then practice on your own writing, and you *will* make progress. Your writing will improve as you begin to understand and incorporate these principles into your work.

EXERCISE **4**

The best work for you to practice on is your own. However, here are a couple of whoppers you can edit to start your warm-up. Rewrite these sentences, cutting out deadwood. Try to shorten them without losing the sense of what they say.

1. Discussions by the participants about the future of the program were conducted over a period of some months in order to determine the validity of the project.

2. The following summarized report has been prepared by the committee to provide a brief and concise review of the actions that have been taken. Only the main points are presented; the details and complete analysis are found in the extensive report that is separately bound.

PRINCIPLE

Use Plain English as an Effective Style for a Broad Audience

To write simply is as difficult as to be good.

Ralph Waldo Emerson

What is "Plain English"? And why is it effective for a broad audience? English is predominantly *teutonic* speech, based on the language of the Angles, the Saxons and the Jutes. When the Normans invaded England in 1066, William the Conqueror made French the language of the English court. In Blackstone's **Commentaries**, the famous 17th century jurist remarks that William's imposition of French was a "badge of foreign servitude and tyranny" on court records and all public proceedings. The tale that William tried to destroy the Saxon tongue is somewhat exaggerated, but there is little doubt that the influx of Norman French into the English language created a bilingualism reflected in the doubling of words in legal documents to this day:

23

- last **will** and **testament** (**will** is Anglo-Saxon; **testament** is French)
- to **give**, **devise** and **bequeath** (**give** and **bequeath** are Anglo-Saxon; **devise** is French)
- transfer of **goods** and **chattels** (**goods** is Anglo-Saxon; **chattels** is French).

English continued as the popular tongue, but French and Latin were studied and promoted as the languages of learning. Interestingly enough, that tradition still exists. As we move on in higher education, we are taught to increase our vocabularies, and this is done largely by learning Latin and French derivatives. However, the basis of everyday, **spoken** English is short, familiar Anglo-Saxon words. Road signs say "STOP" and "GO." They do not say "CEASE" and "PROCEED."

To make matters worse, **lawyers were paid by the word**. Perhaps they still are. Therefore, the tendencies to use abstract and lengthy Norman derivatives, to say the same thing twice, and to write lengthy documents account for the verbosity and pomposity of most legal writing styles. Unfortunately, many non-lawyers imitate this style, thinking that it elevates their writing.

Alan Greenspan, chairman of President Nixon's Council of Economic Advisers, was quoted in the ***Philadelphia Inquirer*** as having testified before a Senate committee in 1974 that:

> It is a tricky problem to find the particular calibration in timing that would be appropriate to stem the acceleration in risk premiums created by falling incomes without prematurely aborting the decline in the inflation-generated risk premiums.[1]

This kind of doublespeak has not significantly hampered Mr. Greenspan's career, possibly because many people think doublespeak sounds impressive. Dan Quayle, when he was Senator from Indiana, explained the need for a Strategic Defense Initiative by saying,

> Why wouldn't an enhanced deterrent, a more stable peace, a better prospect to denying the ones who enter conflict in the first place to have a reduction of offensive systems and an introduction to defensive capability? I believe this is the route the country will eventually go.[2]

Perhaps you think this kind of language characterizes people in political life. But what often happens in corporations is an indoctrination in a different type of doublespeak: language inflated to impress, to make the ordinary seem extraordinary; in other words, to sell ideas or products by dressing them up. A simple car mechanic becomes an

[1]William Lutz, *Doublespeak*, (New York, 1989), p. 5.
[2]*Ibid*, p. 6.

"automotive internist." Black and white TV has "non-multicolor capability." Chrysler "initiates a career alternative enhancement program" and lays off 5,000 workers.

H.W. Fowler, author of *A Dictionary of Modern English Usage*, suggests that there are four preferences that can help you achieve a clear and communicative style:

1. Prefer the short word to the long word.
2. Prefer the Anglo-Saxon word to the Norman word.
3. Prefer the concrete word to the abstract word.
4. Prefer the familiar word to the esoteric word.

The "Plain English" dictionary that follows is based on these preferences. The left-hand column is filled with Norman, abstract polysyllables. The right-hand column contains short, concrete Anglo-Saxon words. Words in the left-hand column contribute to doublespeak, overwhelming your audience with words.

If you have a tendency to overuse words in the left-hand column you may be suffering from *Normanitis*. Now, don't misunderstand me; I am not trying to eliminate those words from your vocabulary completely. I am simply suggesting that you listen to Fowler if your purpose is to communicate clearly. There are times when abstract words and euphemisms are necessary, even desirable: People **perspire**; horses **sweat**. You **disseminate** information, but you **spread** manure.

However, an **idea** is just as good as a **conception**. You can **use** instead of **utilize**; you can **copy** instead of **duplicate**, **try** instead of **endeavor**.

EXERCISE **5**

Look through the dictionary. Identify your own preferences and put a check by them. See which column you favor. If you favor the left column, you probably have "Normanitis."

abbreviate . . . . . . shorten	acknowledge . . . . admit, thank you for
ability . . . . skill	acknowledgment . . answer
accelerate . . . . . . speed up	acquiesce . . . . agree
accommodate . . . . hold, fit, help out	actualize . . . . make real, gain, reach
accompany . . . . . . go (or send) along with	actually . . . . really, in fact
accomplish . . . . . . do, carry out	additional . . . . . . extra, more
accord . . . . agree	adequate . . . . enough
accorded . . . . given	adhere . . . . stick, support
accordingly . . . . . then, thus, therefore	adjacent . . . . near, beside
accumulate . . . . . . collect, gather	adjudge . . . . decide, believe
accrue . . . . add, increase	adjust . . . . set right, reverse, change
achieve . . . . do, carry out	

25

EXERCISE 5
(continued)

administer . . . . . . manage, run, control
advantageous . . . . helpful, profitable, better
advise . . . . tell
aforementioned . . these
albeit . . . . *(avoid this word)*
allow. . . . . let
alternately . . . . . . or
ameliorate . . . . . . improve
and/or . . . . *don't say*: X and/or Y, *say*: X or Y or both
anticipate. . . . . . . expect
apparent . . . . clear
appear. . . . . look, seem
append . . . . attach
appertain. . . . . . . belong, relate
applicable . . . . . apply to
appropriate . . . . suitable
approximately. . . . about, nearly
ascertain . . . . . . find out
assemble . . . . . . meet, gather
assent . . . . agree
assist, assistance . . help, aid
associate . . . . . . join
attain . . . . reach
attempt . . . . try
attributable . . . . due
biannually . . . . . every two years
by means of . . . . by
capable . . . . able
capacity. . . . . . . room, power
category . . . . . . class
cease. . . . . stop
circulate . . . . . . send around
circumscribe. . . . . limit
coalesce. . . . . . . join
cognizant. . . . . . aware
cognizance . . . . . perception, awareness
coincide. . . . . . . fit, agree with
commence . . . . . begin, start
commendable. . . . praiseworthy
commensurate . . . fitting, equal, proper
communication . . . letter, call
compensation . . . . pay
complete . . . . . . finish
components . . . . parts
concede. . . . . . . admit

conceive . . . . . . think, think up
conception. . . . . . idea
concerning . . . . . about
conclude . . . . . . end, settle, decide
concur. . . . . agree
confidence . . . . . trust, belief
consequence. . . . . outcome, result
consequently . . . . then, later
consolidate. . . . . . join, unite, merge, strengthen
construct . . . . . . make, build, put together
constructive . . . . helpful
considerable. . . . . much
continue . . . . . . keep on
converse . . . . . . talk
cooperate. . . . . . work together
correspond. . . . . agree, be like, write
correspondence. . . letter, mail
curtail . . . . cut short, lessen
deficiency . . . . . lack
definitely . . . . . . *(avoid this word)*
deliberate . . . . . think over or think about
deliberation . . . . thought
demonstrate. . . . . show, prove
depreciate . . . . . lose value
design . . . . plan
designation . . . . name
determinate . . . . fixed
devise . . . . plan, invent
dimension . . . . . size, extent
disburse. . . . . . . expend, spend, pay
disclose . . . . . . show
discontinue . . . . stop, give up
disproportional . . . unequal
disregard . . . . . . ignore, overlook
disseminate . . . . spread
dissimilar. . . . . . unlike, different
diversity . . . . . . vary
divide . . . . split, share
duplicate . . . . . . copy
economical. . . . . thrifty, costs little
effectuate. . . . . . carry out
eliminate . . . . . . cut out, get rid of
encounter . . . . . meet, contest
endeavor . . . . . . try
enhance. . . . . . . add to
enumerate . . . . . name, count
equalize. . . . . . . make, equal

equitable . . . . fair
equivalent . . . . . . same, equal
establish . . . . set up
eventuate. . . . . . . happen, occur
evince . . . . show
exigency . . . . need, case
expedient. . . . . . . useful
expedite . . . . hasten
explicit . . . . exact, clear
fabricate . . . . make, build
facilitate . . . . ease, lessen, help
factor . . . . reason, cause
firstly, secondly. . . first, second, etc.
foregoing. . . . . . . this, these
formulate. . . . . . . state, draw up
frequently . . . . . . often
function. . . . . use, work, goal
furthermore . . . . . also, then
generate . . . . make, bring about
gratuitous . . . . . . free
heretofore . . . . . . until now
herewith . . . . with this
hypothesize . . . . . assume, guess
immediately . . . . . at once
implement . . . . . . carry out
inasmuch as . . . . . because
indebtedness . . . . debt
indicate . . . . show
indication. . . . . . . sign
initial . . . . first, original
initiate . . . . begin, start
institute. . . . . begin, set up
irregardless . . . . . *(no such word; use regardless)*
locality . . . . place
maintenance. . . . . upkeep
manifest . . . . show
methodology . . . . procedure
modification. . . . . change, alteration
nevertheless . . . . . but, however, yet
objective . . . . aim
obligate. . . . . bind
obligation . . . . . . debt
optimum . . . . best
participate . . . . . . take part, share
proceed. . . . . go, move along
procure . . . . get, obtain
promulgate . . . . . make known, publish

proficiency. . . . . . skill
purchase . . . . buy
reimburse . . . . . . pay
remuneration . . . . pay, wage, salary
retain . . . . keep
recapitulate . . . . . sum up
said. . . . . *(avoid, as in "the said report")*
satisfy . . . . end, meet, fulfill
secondly . . . . second
secure . . . . get
semiannually . . . . twice a year
signify . . . . mean
similar. . . . . like
similarity . . . . likeness
simultaneously . . . at the same time, together
situated . . . . placed
stabilized . . . . steady, fixed
stationary. . . . . . . fixed, standing
stimulate . . . . spur on, stir up
stringent . . . . strict, tight
subsequent. . . . . . later
subsequently . . . . afterward, later
substantiate . . . . . prove
sufficient . . . . ample, enough, adequate
sufficiently. . . . . . enough
supersede. . . . . . . replace, displace
supervise . . . . oversee
supplement . . . . . add to
support . . . . hold up, bear out, help
surmise . . . . guess, judge
tangible. . . . . real *(or avoid it)*
terminate. . . . . . . end, limit
transact . . . . do, carry on
transform. . . . . . . change, turn
transmit. . . . . send, pass on
transpire . . . . leak out, become known *(transpire doesn't mean " happen")*
ultimate. . . . . last, basic, final
ultimately . . . . . . finally, in the end
utilization . . . . . . use
utilize . . . . use
voluminous . . . . . much, large amount
visualize . . . . see
whereas. . . . . but, while, since
whereby . . . . which

Now let's look at the following phrases. By preferring the right-hand column, you will cut your verbiage a great deal.

along the lines of	like
as of this date	today
as to	about
at this point in time	now
be desirous of	want, need
from the point of view of	for
if and when	if
in behalf of	for
in consideration of	in return for, because of
in order to	to
in terms of	in, for (*or avoid it*)
in the event that	if
in the near future	soon
in the possession of	has, have
in a satisfactory manner	satisfactorily
in and of itself	(*avoid it*)
in the nature of	like
in connection with	toward, to
in relation to	for
in the amount of	for
inasmuch as	because, since
may, or may not	may
more specifically	for example, for instance
on no consideration	never, not at all
on the basis of	by
on the grounds that	since, because
optimize	improve
owing to the fact that	since, because
on the part of	by, among, for
on behalf of	for
on a few occasions	occasionally
prior to	before
provided that	if
refer back to	refer to
subsequent to	after, following
take cognizance of the fact that	see, be aware
take under consideration	consider, think about
take under advisement	consider, think about
the use of	(*avoid it*)
under no circumstances	never
whether or not	whether
with a view to	to
with reference to	about
with regard to	about
with the result that	so that
within the course of	within, during

Another form of doublespeak is **jargon**, the so-called specialized language of a profession or similar group. Sometimes people confuse precise technical language with jargon. *Precise technical language is the shortest, clearest way to communicate within a specialized profession.* A banker can't talk without referring to "assets, liabilities, loan losses," etc. A lawyer needs to use "terms of art." An engineer must talk about "coolant-contaminated cells controlling solenoid valves," and "injector circuit problems."

But these examples of technical language are very different from language that is pretentious, obscure, and esoteric. Jargon makes the simple seem complex. The act of smelling something becomes "organoleptic analysis." Lawyers can either write:

> This lease can be modified and changed only by an instrument in writing signed by the landlord and by the tenant and no surrender of this lease before the expiration of the demised term or any renewal thereof shall be valid unless accepted by the landlord in writing.

or they can write:

> This lease can be changed only by an instrument signed by landlord and tenant. No surrender shall be valid unless accepted by the landlord in writing.

"Expiration of the demised term or any renewal thereof" is jargon, and is compounded by the doubling we spoke of: "modified and changed."

After years of hacking through etymological thickets at the U.S. Public Health Service, a 63-year old official named Philip Broughton hit upon a sure-fire method for converting frustration into fulfillment. Euphemistically called the Systematic Buzz Phrase Projector, Broughton's system employs 30 carefully chosen "buzz-words":

Column 1	Column 2	Column 3
0. integrated	0. management	0. options
1. total	1. organizational	1. flexibility
2. systematized	2. monitored	2. capability
3. parallel	3. reciprocal	3. mobility
4. functional	4. digital	4. programming
5. responsive	5. logistical	5. concept
6. optional	6. transitional	6. time-phase
7. synchronized	7. incremental	7. projection
8. compatible	8. third-generation	8. hardware
9. balanced	9. policy	9. contingency

The procedure is simple. Think of any three-digit number, then select the corresponding buzzword from each column. For instance, number 257 produces "systematized logistical projection", a phrase that can be dropped into virtually any report with that ring of decisive, knowledgeable authority. "No one will have the remotest idea of what you're talking about," says Broughton. "But the important thing is that they're not about to admit it."

EXERCISE **6**

Read these sentences carefully and see if there are any redundancies or unnecessary words. Then make them readable by using Plain English and cutting out deadwood.

1. I attended the April 28, 1988, orientation program and wanted to inform you that I found the information presented to be both informative and extremely well-presented. I have considered how I might be able to participate in this department in future iterations of this conference, and I have determined that I would indeed like to participate.

2. Supplementing our letter of April 15, 1987, please be advised that on April 20, 1987, the District Court of Springfield issued an Execution in the amount of $1,342.70.

3. It is of significant importance that regardless of whether or not an inbound shipment is actually signed and received by the requisition, the University of Connecticut is liable for payment of invoices covered by valid proofs of delivery when these shipments are accepted by a representative of said university.

4. I was unable to secure an answer in my attempt to resolve this question.

5. If your interests are akin to the duties entailed, this could prove to be a very positive and promising step.

6. You will recall that we met in early September to review the department's efforts to integrating women into the decision-making process and to explore possible future activities. While several tentative activities were suggested, we indicated that we wanted to give more thought before determining what could be accomplished.

7. In attempting to determine the strong and weak points of this rating system, we need to understand the structure of the organization. The structure of the organization is the key in determining what control system is best suited for that operation and hence an appropriate rating system.

PRINCIPLE

Follow the Guidelines for Readability

You might ask: If "Plain English" is a fine style for a broad audience, why can't I use it all the time?

Some people do, especially those individuals who understand the **guidelines for readability**. Plain English is not just the choice of words; **it is an effort to help the reader**. Short sentences can help. Short paragraphs can also help. Using enough white space is another factor in making a document readable. Following these guidelines, you will avoid the most common characteristic of mediocre writing: "chunky" prose. Chunky prose is just that — a chunk of words, an unbroken paragraph. It's a little like serving up a meal of nothing but mashed potatoes. No meat, no vegetable, no dessert — just starch.

Guidelines for Readability

1. Avoid long sentences (average 3 lines).
2. Avoid long paragraphs (average 8 lines).
3. Use simple, direct sentences. Keep subjects close to verbs.

✗ 4. Punctuate properly. *Rules pg 237-243*

✗ 5. Use white space and layout to help the eye of the reader.

    a. Use a serif type and make it large enough (no smaller than this).

    b. Avoid right-justified margins. They can get monotonous.

6. Use lists whenever appropriate.

7. Use topic headings to make appropriate separations (background from foreground, actions from conditions, problems from solutions, findings from options, recommendations from remarks, etc.).

✗ 8. Use "Plain English" or standard English whenever possible.

Below is a "before and after" example of chunky prose. The "before" violates the guidelines for readability, while the "after" uses headings to address what the reader needs to know.

Before

Reengineering is the buzzword of the day in corporate America.

What is reengineering? It is the radical redesign of business systems and has been embraced and enthusiastically practiced by most large American corporations. It focuses on quality and customer relations, contrary to the prior practice of concentrating on productivity. The difference is simple. When the focus was on productivity, customer concerns and quality were often ignored. Countries such as Japan and Germany learned during their rebuilding years following World War II that the keys to success in the years ahead were to focus on quality and customer satisfaction. The United States learned this lesson very late, as we were "the only game in town" during the postwar years, and little attention was paid to quality considerations. As world economies grew, so did the demand for U.S. products.

A gentleman by the name of W. Edward Deming tried to encourage U.S. companies to focus on the consumer and pay attention to quality. He was largely ignored. He then took his message to Japan and, as they say, the rest is history. The Japanese underwent a dramatic paradigm shift. Where their production had once been known to be "junk" and "cheap" and "low-tech," they had transformed themselves into producing products that were high-quality, expensive and very high tech. Americans had been caught by surprise, and we have been trying to catch up ever since. Reengineering is the tool that we are using to turn ourselves around.

We recognize now that our processes and systems were outdated, that in many cases we had merely automated bad manual systems, thinking that speed (and productivity) was the answer. Our companies are not flexible enough to meet the demands of better educated and more demanding consumers and we are seeing the results everywhere. Dramatic change is what we need, and corporate reengineering is a means to that end.

After

What Is Reengineering?
It's a radical change in the way corporate America does business.

What Does It Do?
It calls for a shift from the old-time American business practice of just meeting productivity goals to a broader emphasis on delivering high-quality products and services and maintaining excellent customer relations.

Where Has It Been Successful?
Business visionaries in post-World War II Japan and Germany recognized that the key to success was to focus on product quality and customer satisfaction. The worldwide demand for high-quality, high-tech German and Japanese products over American products speaks for itself.

Lessons from the Past?
Contrary to popular belief, the focus on quality and consumer satisfaction was not born in Japan. After the war, W. Edward Deming tried to encourage U.S. companies to focus on quality and consumer loyalty. He was largely ignored. He then took his message to Japan and, as they say, the rest is history.

It's Not Too Late to Change!
The worldwide demand for high-quality German and Japanese products caught America by surprise. But we now recognize that our processes and systems have not kept up with a changing world. Our companies are not flexible enough to meet the demands of better-educated and more demanding consumers, and we are seeing the results everywhere. Corporate America must embrace reengineering if it hopes to compete in the new world economies.

See what happens when you apply the guidelines for readability to the following excerpt. You have an entirely different impression between "before and after". Once again, I have annotated with the number of the main principle that is violated.

Before

1. <u>At the present time</u> *(violates #4)*, she <u>has been entered</u> *(violates #9)* on our list to take the Basic Accounting Course, and we will notify her when she is eligible to take the course.

2. <u>In regard to our conversations by telephone recently</u> *(violates #4)*, I am enclosing copies of chapters concerning taxes from two public utility textbooks. One book <u>was written by</u> *(violates #4)* Foster and Rodey; the last printing was June, 1954. The other book was written by Mr. James E. Suelflow and the last printing was in 1974. Even though these two texts were printed approximately twenty years apart <u>they read essentially the same way in regard to the subject of</u> *(violates #2 and #5)* accounting for taxes.

3. <u>It is our understanding that</u> *(violates #10)* the CPAs have explained what actions, documentation and records are needed to eliminate the deficiencies that presently exist in the Telephone Authority accounting system. We further understand that the REA Operations Field Representative has been providing advice and assistance to Telephone Authority personnel <u>in the area of establishment of continuing property records</u> *(violates #4)*. All possible efforts should be continued to assure that the accounting system, records, and procedures <u>are brought</u> *(violates #9)* to a level of adequacy that will enable the financial statements <u>to be audited and certified</u> *(violates #9)*.

(199 words)

After

1. She is on our list for the Basic Accounting Course; we'll notify her as soon as she's eligible to take it.

2. I'm enclosing copies of tax chapters from two public utility textbooks — one by Foster and Rodey (June, 1954), and one by James E. Suelflow (1974). Despite the twenty years that separate them, they both confirm what I told you about accounting for taxes.

3. To allow the CPAs to audit and certify your financial statements, you must bring your accounting system, records, and procedures up to standard as quickly as possible. We understand that the CPAs have explained how to do this, and that the REA Operations Representative has been helping your personnel establish continuing property records.

(118 words)

EXERCISE **7**   **Now, apply the guidelines for readability to the following examples of "chunky" prose.**

1. Community-supported day-care facilities are often needed in neighborhoods having many working women with small children, or families with no father in the household. The income level of the neighborhood has bearing too, since families with higher incomes can more easily afford adequate private care. Several kinds of useful information about neighborhoods can be found in census reports, such as the number of working mothers who live with their husbands and have children under six years old, the number of families with incomes below the poverty level without a father present, and the average number of children under 6 years old in such families. This kind of information can help in estimating how many mothers might be interested in a day-care center, how many children might be involved, and where the best location would be.

2. We have expended considerable effort in developing an effective certification plan for our four nuclear plant simulators. The program has been designed to both provide for initial certification, addressing the specific requirements of the Nuclear Regulatory Commission, and to ensure ongoing compliance with the requirements of the Connecticut Health and Safety Board. Our plan for ensuring ongoing compliance with NRC regulations is centered around a formal, proceduralized Certification Program that addresses, as one of its main functions, simulator configuration management. Simulator configuration management will remain an ongoing commitment requiring considerable attention and allocation of resources throughout the life of the simulator. The Certification process concentrates on updating of the design database, implementation of plant design changes, resolution of simulator deficiencies, performance testing, and documentation.

Guidelines for Listing

We cannot talk about readability without mentioning a powerful technique to help the reader grasp meaning quickly. That technique is **listing**. We tend to have a prejudice for the prose paragraph, even when it is inappropriate. We rarely think of using lists in business writing, because no one taught us in college how to make lists or how helpful they can be. What follows are guidelines for listing that illustrate the principles involved. Although they are not rigid, don't ignore any of them casually:

1. Use a full sentence, ending in a colon, for the introductory statement preceding the list.

   - Sentence fragments can be confusing in an introductory statement.

2. Separate the action steps from comments, examples, or other explanatory material.

   - This list provides a good example.

3. List each item separately.

   - If you combine two actions in one sentence, as in a cookbook style, the reader may easily miss one action.

4. List the steps in a sequence that is logical to the reader.

   - We are writing for the reader, not ourselves.

5. Write each step as a full sentence, preferably beginning the step with an action verb.

6. Be parallel in style throughout the list.

   - For example: if you use an action verb to start the first two items in the list, then use it to start all other items.

7. Be consistent in word choice.

   - Avoid unnecessary synonyms. Consciously repeat key words, so as not to confuse the reader.

8. Avoid the passive voice.

   - Most people overwork the passive voice.

In this "before and after," see how listing techniques make for a far more readable document.

Before

SUBJECT: Scrap Report — What has it told NAPC

Attached are some statistics that were taken from the scrap report as it is presently being reported. The figures may be in question but they express the magnitude of the problems at NAPC from a scrap point of view. The dollar values are based on the sales price of the boards. The top ten customers from the last six months are listed in exhibit 1. The top ten customers were only 12% of the total scrap, so the idea of working on particular problem part numbers wouldn't really affect the overall scrap rate.

The top ten defects for the last six months, listed in exhibit 2, are 60% of the total scrap. This list presents a real opportunity to lower the scrap at NAPC. The number one defect is lamination defects, which already has an improvement team working on it. They have made significant progress but due to the magnitude of the problem, it will take a long time to solve. The team has a 40% drop in reported lamination defects since April of this year. The next biggest problems are opens. The improvement team has decreased the escapes to under 100 ppm. This is very good, because now our customers don't see the problems. Although the problems are still occurring, NAPC is doing a better job screening them.

Exhibit 3 shows an estimation of the dollars scrapped at NAPC per day, per week, and per month. At the present rate of scrap, NAPC will scrap by years end $3.6 million with approximately $14,000.00 scrapped per working day. That's a lot of money going to the dump every day. Even if the actual figure is half that, it is still a lot of money. Hopefully the TQM improvement teams in the two plants with the right direction will impact on these problems and find causes and implement solutions.

After

SUBJECT: Scrap Report – What has it told NAPC?

The attached statistics from the scrap report reveal to NAPC the magnitude of the problems. The dollar values are based on the sales price of the boards.

Exhibit 1:
(a)   The top ten customers of the last six months equal 12% of total scrap.
(b)   Working on a particular problem part's numbers won't affect the overall scrap rate.

Exhibit 2:
(a)   The top ten defects for the last six months are 60% of the total scrap.
(b)   This list presents an opportunity to lower the scrap rate.
(c)   The number one defect is lamination.
(d)   There is an improvement team working on this difficult problem. Since April, they've achieved a 40% drop in lamination defects.
(e)   The improvement team has solved the problems of opens by decreasing the escape to less than 100 ppm.
(f)   Even though our customers don't see the problems, they are still occurring.

Exhibit 3: An estimate of dollars scrapped per day, week and month.
By the end of 1991, the scrap will total $3.6 million with $14,000 scrapped each working day. That is a lot of money going to the dump.

EXERCISE **8** **Apply the guidelines for listing to the following block paragraph. Try to make this more accessible to the eye of the reader. Make the important information stand out.**

Job Description: Budget Analyst

I assist the Budget Officer in the full range of budget management for the Office of the Secretary as well as other independent agencies administered by the Office of the Secretary. I am responsible for the consolidation of information, requests, program evaluation, analysis, and review of operating elements of the Secretariat, as well as other independent agencies. This requires in-depth study of programs to determine future year impact, useful payoff of resources, priority of programs or needs for allocation of functions. I review program estimates, narrative and statistical material to ensure adequacy of submission, support of Departmental and Administration objectives, and provide for the best possible usage of dollars and positions requested. I assist in the planning and development of material for presentation to the Assistant Secretary, Policy, Budget, and Administration, Departmental Budget Office, Office of Management and Budget and Congressional review. I participate in the entire process of funds control for assigned areas: planning, apportionment, allocation, allotment, analysis, and forecasting requirements. I review all monthly operating and forecast reports to determine adequacy of funding and to anticipate possible violations. I prepare reports as may be required by the Departmental Budget Office, OMB, Congress of the Assistant Secretary, Policy, Budget and Administration. I review all functions of the Working Capital Fund to determine acceptable operating levels, financial condition and recommend appropriate action in regard to future operations of the fund.

Use Parallelism in Lists and in Sentences

Many people do not deserve good writing, they are so pleased with bad.

Ralph Waldo Emerson

This principle is related to listing but is broader in scope. Parallelism suggests that when ideas are equal, you should reflect that equality by embodying the ideas in similar grammatical structures. In other words, "apples and oranges" are both nouns joined by *and* which reflects equality. "Lying and cheating" are both present participles. "To live and to die" are both infinitives.

The easiest way to see this principle is in a **listing** format (refer to page 36 for the Guidelines for Listing). Since all the items in a list should be *equal* in status, you should use the same grammatical structure for each item. If you begin with active verbs, stay with active verbs. If you begin with complete sentences, stay with complete sentences. If you begin with fragments, stick with fragments. Of course, if you don't know an infinitive from a participle, it's hard to practice parallelism.

The following list is easy to follow because it conforms to the principle of parallelism:

SUBJECT: Supplemental 1989 W-2
ISSUE: Your 1989 W-2 is wrong. Salary and deductions for one or more pay periods were excluded.

OUR RESPONSIBILITY:

- To provide a supplemental W-2 showing additional earnings
- To provide a letter of explanation to accompany your tax returns
- To provide reimbursement for any additional charge by your tax preparer upon receipt of a paid invoice
- To establish controls to prevent future problems of this nature.

YOUR RESPONSIBILITY:

1. If you **have** filed your 1989 tax returns:

   - File amended tax returns including the additional earnings
   - Attach letter of explanation to amended returns.

2. If you **have not** filed your 1989 tax returns:

   - File Form 4868 "Application for Automatic Extension to File U.S. Individual Tax Return" (Copy attached)
   - Pay estimated taxes with Form 4868
   - File similar forms and pay estimated taxes to state or city taxing authorities
   - Attach letter of explanation to final tax returns.

EXERCISE **9**

Study the "before and after" example. Then rewrite the three lists below to make them parallel. There is no *one* right way to fix these sentences. But remember, if you start with nouns, stick with nouns. If you start with verbs, stick with verbs.

Before	**After**
The new software:	The new software:
• receives customer calls.	• receives customer calls.
• provide design assistance.	• provides design assistance.
• challenging to the user.	• challenges the user.

1. The job responsibilities include:

   • accurate and timely processing of mortgage collection reports from assigned correspondents and weekly corrections to transactions processed and rejected

   • monthly billings audited for accuracy of balances and installments with corrections noted before mailing

   • corresponds with office regarding discrepancies and resolves problems associated with accurate processing of reports or other related matters

2. Property insurance provides:

   • coverage is on an "all risks" basis (versus named perils)

   • brings all local policies to a company standard

   • the current $50 million limit will increase to $75 million on Dec. 1st

   • $25,000 deductible, if there is no local coverage in place

     Example — If lightning damage is not covered under your local policy, the master policy provides the coverage subject to a $25 thousand deductible.

3. Some of the key facts of XYZ Corporation are:

   • world's largest manufacturer of widgets, wadgets, and gizmos

   • revenues $3.6 billion in 1992

   • more than 75% of revenues for 1992 were generated outside the U.S.

   • employs 50,000 people worldwide

   • global presence — 30 manufacturing facilities in 19 countries with products sold in 163 of the world's 171 nations

   • 1700 service locations worldwide

In addition to parallelism in lists, you should also use parallelism in sentences when there are ideas of equal value.

Examples of Parallel Structure

1. We hold these truths to be self-evident: *that* all men are created equal; *that* they are endowed by their creator with certain unalienable rights; *that* among these are life, liberty and the pursuit of happiness.

2. *Ask not* what your country can do for you; *ask* what you can do for your country.

3. *To err* is human; *to forgive*, divine.

4. *Give me* liberty or *give me* death.

5. These extremists feed on fear, hate and terror. They have *no* program for America, *no* program for the Republican Party. They have *no* solution for our problems of chronic unemployment, of education, of agriculture, or racial injustice or strife.

   On the contrary, *they* spread distrust. *They* engender suspicion. *They* encourage disunity. And *they* operate from the dark shadows of secrecy.

   There is *no* place in this Republican Party for *such* hawkers of hate, *such* purveyors of prejudice, *such* fabricators of fear, whether Communist, Ku Klux Klan or Birchers.

   There is *no* place in this Republican Party for those who would infiltrate its ranks, distort its aims, and convert it into a cloak of apparent respectability for a dangerous extremism.

   These people have nothing in common with Republicanism. *These people have nothing in common* with Americanism. The Republican Party must repudiate these people.

EXERCISE **10** **Now let's rewrite some sentences that violate parallelism. How can you fix them?**

1. We were affected by the uncertainty of their policy on outside contacts and to what degree they were to pursue information from outside contacts without causing problems for the company.

2. The project will be collating existing approaches to strategic decision making in enterprise, forming public policy, and program management. It will also identify the more useful and practical concepts and approaches for developing countries. And it needs to evaluate new approaches to further development.

3. A project of this type might support our work with food and agriculture policy, agricultural planning, effectiveness analysis for other programs such as health and nutrition, and for tailoring administrative reform opportunities when they arise.

4. Our personnel provide support to the educational system via tutoring local students, assisting teachers in business encounters, and employee involvement with local school systems and boards of education.

5. There is no doubt that we need to work on several weaknesses: improving our free-throw percentage, better all-around shot selection, tighten up our man-to-man defense.

6. Donna (Legal Assistant of our litigation team along with myself) is responsible for the accuracy and integrity of all the data loaded in the system and assisting in identifying current and future needs of the departments supported by the system.

Use Vivid Verbs to Give Your Sentences Force

If your verbs are weak and your syntax rickety, your sentences will fall apart.

William Zinsser

In addition to using Plain English whenever it's appropriate and thinking of the reader by following the guidelines for readability, there is another factor that is all-important in making sentences forceful, clear, precise and brief. That principle is: **use vivid verbs.**

The verb is the heart of your sentence:

Example: The traffic moved very slowly along the highway.

• The traffic **crawled**, **crept**, **inched**, etc.

The first sentence isn't wrong, but it isn't vivid or precise.

For example, in the following sentence we see a lengthy verb form "is involved in the reorganization of several departments."

> The middle management of Pan American is involved in the reorganization of several departments necessitated by the introduction of the IBM computer system.

What is the <u>action</u>? Somebody is reorganizing. So in the rewrite, we need to find a subject and a verb and then create a simple, declarative sentence.

> Pan American is reorganizing several departments.

But we also have to ask ourselves what "necessitates" is about. We know that necessity is a causation word, so why not go for "because"?

> Because of our new IBM computer system, Pan American is reorganizing several departments.

Now, let's look at the following sentence:

> This was taken into consideration by the committee prior to the committee's recommendation of the change.

Later (in Principle 10), we will talk about the passive voice, which makes your style flaccid and confusing. For now, let's look at the verb "was taken into consideration." Who is the actor? Who did what to whom? The committee, of course. And what did it do? It <u>considered</u>. Let's turn all the verbs into active, vivid forms. This will make for a more forceful sentence. So now it should read:

> The committee considered this before recommending the change.

Let's look at one more example:

> There are no significant changes for the month of December in regard to staff.

The "to be" verb construction is not active. Let's put some action into this sentence.

> The staff did not change.

But what about "significant"? Let's turn that into an adverb: "significantly."

Without the passive verb and all the deadwood we have:

> The staff did not change significantly in December.

EXERCISE **11** **Look at the weak verb constructions in the following sentences. Change them into vivid, strong verbs that emphasize the *action* of the sentence. I have underlined the weakest verbs.**

1. It <u>should be kept</u> in mind that whenever a particular exposure warrants Loss Prevention services, an attempt <u>would be made</u> to arrange a visit with the appropriate Loss Prevention individual <u>to assist</u> in the control of the problem.

2. The purpose of this pilot program <u>is to begin to address</u> the needs of banks <u>to respond to</u> a wide variety of needs that offset the economic development of a neighborhood, a community, or the region as a whole.

3. The preparation of middle managers for more substantial tasks <u>has always been difficult</u> for institutions.

As you can see from the following example, it is also very important in technical writing that you use vivid verbs, crisp sentences, and ample white space to aid the eye of the reader.

Before

From Figures 1 through 5 <u>it can be concluded that</u> excellent correlation of theoretical calculations of modal damping with test data measurements is possible, using the 1983 analysis. The analytical <u>results obtained with</u> the 1982 analysis <u>do not differ significantly from</u> the 1983 analysis results except at high values of collective pitch when blade lift stall effects become quite important. The effect of stall on hovering performance <u>is illustrated in</u> Figure 11 which shows that the rotor lift calculated by the 1983 analysis is less than that for the 1982 analysis; the difference in lift becomes significant for collective pitches above 20 degrees as the rotor experiences stall. The effect of lift stall and compressibility on tail rotor stability is clearly manifested in Figure 1 for the blade symmetric flatwise mode. The 1983 analysis shows a reduction in modal damping for pitch values beyond 20 degrees that is in agreement with the general behavior of the test data.

After

Figures 1–5 show that test data correlate well with the 1983 theoretical calculations of modal damping. Those calculations <u>scarcely differ</u> from the 1982 results except at high collective pitch when effects of blade lift stall become important.

As Figure 11 indicates, the 1983 analysis, by calculating how stall affects hovering, found less rotor lift than the 1982 analysis did. As the rotor stalls, the difference in lift <u>becomes significant</u> for collective pitches above 20 degrees.

Figure 1 shows how lift stall and compressibility affect tail rotor stability for the blade symmetric flatwise mode. A reduction in modal damping for pitches above 20 degrees <u>matches the test data</u>, according to the 1982 analysis.

EXERCISE **12** **Shorten the following sentences and tighten them up with vivid verbs that focus the action.**

1. This is something that may or may not be of interest to Stu as he performs his analysis of the various quotes.

2. The United States and the Soviet Union are found to be in agreement with the general principles of German re-unification.

3. After consulting with Sales, I have arrived at a decision to reduce the inventory of Wacky Wall Walkers in our Kalamazoo branch.

4. It has been decided to make adjustments to the spring tension in all of our P-38 electric swizzle sticks.

5. Would you please make out a list of all the purple and green imitation lizard watchbands that also have the brass-plated buckles?

6. The difference between our improved market share this year and last is due to the fact that absenteeism is down and production is up.

7. 1989 has been a year of problem definition.

8. In his speech to the Board, the CEO said that our commitment is to contain the growth in inventory backlogs.

9. The transfer of assets will be made today.

10. At the request of the Purchasing Department, we have done a review of the Master File listing.

11. This letter is a follow-up to our phone conversation yesterday.

12. We have done the benefit calculations for the July monthly report.

13. This decision to change the Connecticut General position is the result of much investigation.

PRINCIPLE

Avoid Verbs in the Passive Voice

Just get it down on paper and then we'll see what to do with it.
Maxwell Perkins

Having focused on using vivid verbs, we should not assume that this principle is the only answer. There are other aspects to verbs that can help create clear, forceful sentences.

First, we'll look at **active versus passive voice**. A passive verb fits into the following pattern: first, it uses a form of the verb "to be" and then a past participle of the main verb.

Passive Sentences

Subject	Verb "to be"	Participle	"By" (actor)
I	am	pleased	by your cooperation
He	is	seen	by every visitor
It	was	needed	by the Company
They	were	transferred	by the Agency
She	had been	sent	by the Director

Here are the <u>same</u> sentences switched to the active voice. You will notice that the switch comes about when the actor becomes the subject of the sentence.

Active Sentences

- Your cooperation pleases me.
- Every visitor sees him.
- The Company needed it.
- The Agency transferred them.
- The Director had sent her.

You can see that active verbs make sentences shorter, clearer, and more direct. Sometimes sentences with passive verbs don't name the actor. Nevertheless, an actor is implied.

"That report will not be needed." **By whom?**
I, we, the committee will not need the report.

"The statistics were compiled." **By whom?**
I, we, the company compiled the statistics.

There **are** times when the passive voice is appropriate. For instance, if the subject is truly passive, your sentence should reflect that fact: **He was laid to rest.**

Or it might be that the actor is unknown or unimportant: **His car was stolen in the middle of the night.**

A third case involves deliberately hiding from responsibility: **According to the White House, mistakes were made.**

EXERCISE **13** **Look through the following sentences. Are there any justifiable passives? Which ones are they and why? Now change the unnecessary passives to active voice.**

1. A review of the technical considerations for pump operation **was performed**.

2. Action **is being taken** to replace the outdated computers.

3. The OMB Director **was amazed** by the rate of progress.

4. According to a company spokesman, over 3,000 employees **will be laid off** in November.

5. The intervals **will be determined** by a programmable calculator.

6. One set of sample questions **is included** for your use.

7. Emphasis **will be placed** upon studying the impact at the Branch Office level.

8. A separate form **is to be attached** to each policy endorsement so that every transaction will produce a separate form.

9. The information **was provided** by Ginny.

10. The switchboard **was swamped** with calls demanding the CEO's resignation.

11. A three month study **was taken** of all incoming Bills of Lading.

12. A list **was drawn up** (and checked twice) to see who was naughty or nice.

PRINCIPLE

Use Direct Address (Speak Directly to the Reader)

Anything that helps you imagine you're talking to someone helps your writing.

Jonathan Price

A similar form to the passive voice is "indirect address," and it has several sources. Perhaps the most common is the belief that, by removing the "I" from a piece of writing, the author sounds less egotistical.

A second source reflects the writing of American scientists who feel that objectivity rather than subjectivity should be stressed. Therefore, "I" (the subjective observer) never appears. "It" (the impersonal, objective observer) becomes the subject of the sentence ("It should be noted that tryptophane hydrochloride produces spurious side effects when…").

The tendency to allow some God-like, impersonal observer to make notes rather than a human or team of humans is a difficult attitude to eliminate both in scientific and bureaucratic prose. Hiding behind indirect address does not magically grant objective truth to a document; it **does** make it harder to read and saps it of clarity and precision.

In Plain English, we speak directly to the reader by:

1. Using words that refer to **people**:
   - Pronouns — I, we, you, they...
   - Masculine and feminine nouns — Mr. Hernandez, Ms. Olivetti, the salesman, our secretary...
   - The word "people"

2. Asking **direct** questions:
   "Have you finished the study yet?"

3. Making **direct** requests or giving **direct** orders:
   "Please have the study ready when we meet today."
   "Can you finish the project by the 3rd of June?"

EXERCISE **14** **Rewrite the following sentences to eliminate indirect address. Remember, you want to speak directly from one human being to another. Make other improvements where necessary – for instance, cut out deadwood, use active verbs, etc.**

1. During the meeting it was decided that the direction of the study should be toward special files, not W.C. files.

2. It must be recognized, however, that his sources were often dated.

3. It was thought that an analyst could communicate effectively over the phone and an occasional visit to New York may be required.

4. It should also be noted that this suggestion was made by the team early in the report process.

5. It was indicated that this product has been placed on the market since they first started this firm.

6. It is planned that all the products will be distributed by 1995.

7. It is recommended that a team be included in the final evaluation.

8. It appears that the level of responsibility for specific technical functions is markedly lower than what I feel is required by our organizational structure and circumstances.

9. It was noted that voltage or reactive performance in this time frame might undergo significant changes.

10. It is suggested that the group be comprised of 4 to 6 regular members and some number of liaison members.

11. With this functional arrangement, it is intended that the time commitment for any degree of an individual's group participation should be minimal.

12. It is planned that all the products will be distributed by the company.

11

P R I N C I P L E

Avoid Nominals

The difference between the right word and the almost right is the difference between lightning and the lightning bug.

Mark Twain

Nominals are verbs made into nouns that name the act the verb stands for. Nominalized verbs often end in **-tion, -ment, -ance, -ing, -al**, or **-ure**. Here are some examples:

Verb	Nominal	Verb	Nominal
to procure	procurement	to attend	attendance
to fail	failure	to provide	provision
to submit	submission	to comply	compliance
to conclude	conclusion	to give	giving
to remove	removal	to inflate	inflation

There are three principal problems with nominals.

1. Nominals, like the passive voice, push the real actor out of the subject slot. This generally makes the sentence less clear and less direct:

Before	With Nominals
John decided the case quickly.	**John's decision of the case was quick.**
	The decision of the case by John was quick.

2. Nominals, like the passive, can lead the writer to leave out the real "actor" altogether:

Before	With Nominals
John decided the case quickly.	**The decision of the case was quick.**

3. Nominals can leave out the original verb and the subject:

Before	With Nominals
After notifying the State,	**After notice to the State was given,**
John suspended the grant.	**a suspension was granted.**

The result is a telegraphic style that <u>sometimes</u> can be useful, but too often places an unfair burden on the reader to fill in the missing terms.

The worst case of "nominalitis" I've worked with was an executive who had difficulty communicating with his superiors. Every other word he spoke was abstract, ending in "ion." I asked him to free-associate verbally and he proceeded to speak of "direction… confusion… completion… satisfaction… nutrition…"

"Whoa," I said. "Stick with **nutrition**. Do you see anything? Taste anything? Be specific."

"Corn-on-the-cob," he answered.

"Great. What else?"

"Butter… melting… savory… sweet… "

"Excellent! Now I begin to understand you."

From then on, he saw the power of ordinary, concrete language. His superiors no longer complain about his abstract communications. His responsibilities, job title, and salary have all increased.

EXERCISE **15** **Rewrite the following sentences, changing the nominals back into strong, active verbs. See how this improves the power of the sentences.**

1. We would like to encourage your submission of a bid for the new contract. Compliance with bidding guidelines is required.

2. The inflation of the actual costs by our accounting office has led to many angry memos from within the company.

3. The attendance of you and your staff at the next sales meeting would be greatly appreciated.

4. It is tempting to draw the conclusion that all Savings and Loans are unsafe, but nothing could be more wrong. Any failure on our part to correct this false impression would be remiss.

PRINCIPLES OF

STRUCTURE

12

PRINCIPLE

Empathize with Your Readers; Help Them Find Your Meaning

I try to leave out the parts that people skip.

Elmore Leonard

This principle sounds easy. In fact, it is one of the most difficult of all the principles because so many of us are unable to put ourselves into the shoes, minds, ears and eyes of another. This becomes more difficult when we have multiple readers we do not know.

In addition, modern linguistic theory suggests that instead of receiving meaning when we read, we actually create meaning. Depending upon our experience, our education, our mind sets, or our conceptual frameworks, we will react differently to the same words on a page. If a business letter begins with comments about the weather ("We have had a lovely August"), Westerners might find the communication frustrating, whereas business people in Japan would understand that such talk is an effort to establish a friendly and harmonious relationship.

But even without the cultural difference, a person who receives a memo that says "Please feel free to contact me" might react differently if he or she were the CEO. That person might call you up and say, "You're damn right I feel free to contact you!"

Throughout this book we focus on how you can help your reader *see* and ***understand*** exactly what you intend. We know that clarity and brevity will help. We also know that there are many typographical devices that help the reader see meaning. If your thoughts flow logically, you should also be able to guide the reader with transitional words and phrases. But most important of all, you must provide a structure for the reader, a skeleton upon which all the words rest.

If you were fortunate enough to have a teacher who demanded noun topic outlines in an alphanumeric system (I, A, B, i, a, b, etc.), you probably still follow that format religiously. Lately there has been much emphasis on writing the "natural" way, using the right side of the brain to flow in an unimpeded stream of associations. This method encourages thoughtful abundance. My own preference is a logic tree. It does not freeze your thoughts the way a noun-topic outline can (study the exhibit on the next page). Even more fluid is the technique of mind mapping.[3] Regardless of the system you choose, these frames or "skeletons" are tools to create **form**.

Figure 12-1 — Drawing a Conclusion

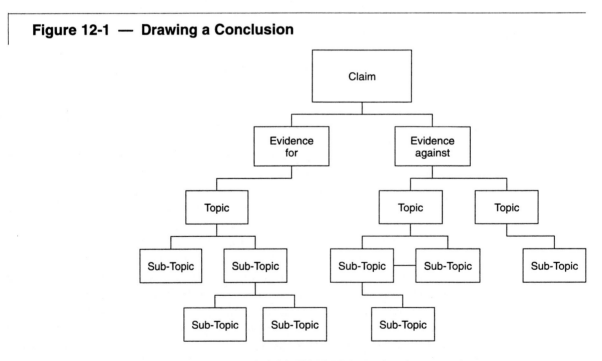

LOGIC TREES help focus your ideas.

---

[3]An excellent book on the subject is *Mind Mapping* by Joyce Wycoff, (New York, 1991).

Figure 12-2 — Space Suit Design

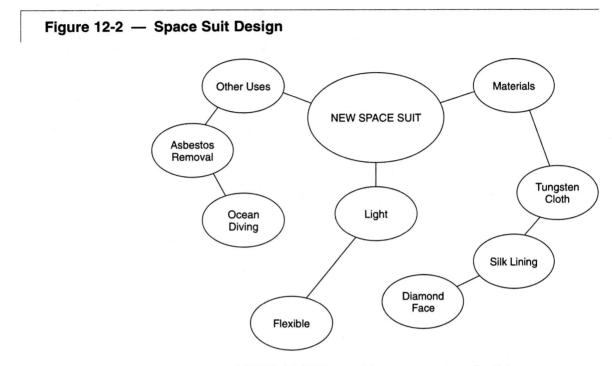

MIND MAPS are a shortcut to more flexible,
stream-of-consciousness, creative thinking.

The Résumé

There are many prescribed forms in business writing. These provide a ready-made structure, and you will be practicing these forms in your homework assignments. You will be writing progress reports and problem/solution memos, analyses and option papers, executive summaries and formal reports, procedures and proposals. However, we will begin with a form that concerns you immediately, a form you need to labor over to understand what it says about you. That form is the résumé.

To write an excellent résumé, you have to understand your reader. No résumé can serve for all types of employment. However, the résumé is a general statement about you. Each job that you apply for may involve a different emphasis. *The purpose of your letter of application is to define more specifically what points in your résumé would be particularly attractive to a specific employer.* Recruiters do read these application letters carefully. It helps them determine if you're right for their company.

Rest assured, the application letter and the résumé should be seen as persuasive documents. You want to knock the socks off a potential employer. You want that employer to want <u>you</u>.

At this stage in your life, you may not have difficulty keeping your résumé brief and clear. But when you start to write your résumé, what kind of reader do you visualize? In the first stage of composition, you should probably imagine someone in a personnel office who has to look at hundreds of résumés each week. That person is looking for ways to disqualify most applicants so that he or she can choose the one or two people who are "worth" an interview.

If you are chosen, this will involve a visit to the employer's site. Then you're faced with a different kind of audience, a department head. In general, you want to show that you are capable, responsible and pleasant. Depending upon your specialty, you want first to emphasize the experience that proves you are capable of doing the type of job you're applying for.

You have to be very clear about what you want to do. The reader will be looking at the résumé to see if your experience fits what you want. If you have had extensive work experience, you may want to present a **functional résumé** that emphasizes the on-the-job accomplishments of your past experience.

Whatever pattern you choose, your name should go at the top. Then put the most important information first. That information has to hold the reader's attention. If you've had little work experience, you'll stress your education. If you've had extensive experience, you'll lead with that topic.

Brief summary for résumés and application letters

1. Empathize with your readers. Think about what *they* need to know.
2. Be clear about what you want to do.
3. Put the most important information first.
4. Highlight your accomplishments.
5. Try to keep the résumé to one page unless you have years of experience full of outstanding accomplishments.
6. Be accurate, but you have no obligation to share information that will hurt you.
7. Use a format and typeset that pleases the eye.
8. Direct your résumé and letter toward **results**.
9. Research the company(s) you are considering.
10. Market yourself with dynamic job search letters.

11. Send a thank-you letter to everyone who interviews you.
12. Name and explain experiences that describe your character strengths.

E X E R C I S E **16** **The following examples should provide you with a starting point for your own résumé. Notice the improvements in the "before and after" résumé by Joan Smith. After studying these examples, write your own general résumé.**

Before

JOAN B. SMITH

123 Walnut Grove
Storrs, CT 06268
(203) 429-1234

OBJECTIVE	A challenging entry level position.
EDUCATION 5/92	THE UNIVERSITY OF CONNECTICUT, Storrs, CT Bachelor of Science in Business Administration Major: Finance
EXPERIENCE 5/91	Résumés Plus, Storrs, CT Typist Processed and maintained client files. Typed documents.
3/91 – 9/91	American Eagle, Manchester, CT Sales Associate (part-time) Met sales goals. Assisted in the execution of floor moves and display changes. Customer service.
9/90 – 5/91	Athletic Communications, UConn, Storrs, CT Administrative Assistant Clerical responsibilities
5/90 – 8/90	Department of Residential Life, UConn, Storrs, CT Assistant Supervisor / Guest Liaison Assisted Conference Hall Supervisor with information processing. Processed campus-wide routine and emergency maintenance calls.
COMPUTER	DOS, WordPerfect, Microsoft Word, Lotus 1-2-3, and dBASE III Plus.
INTERESTS	Sailing, swimming, aerobics, piano, and ice skating.
REFERENCES	Available on request.

After

JOAN B. SMITH

123 Walnut Grove
Storrs, CT 06268
(203) 429-1234

OBJECTIVE   A position requiring my financial, analytical and communication
skills.

EDUCATION   THE UNIVERSITY OF CONNECTICUT   Storrs, CT
Bachelor of Science in Business Administration, May 1992
Major: Finance

EXPERIENCE   RÉSUMÉS PLUS   Storrs, CT
May 1991 –   *Summer Manager / Word Processor*
Present   Operated business in owner's absence. Processed and maintained
client files. Typed documents ranging from one-page résumés to 300+
page theses. Maintained high level of customer service.

Mar 1991 –   AMERICAN EAGLE, Buckland Hills Mall   Hartford, CT
Sep 1991   *Sales Associate* (part-time)
Met and exceeded sales goals consistently. Assisted in floor moves
and display changes according to store standards. Maintained high
level of customer service. Accepted manager-trainee responsibilities.

Sep 1990 –   UCONN ATHLETIC COMMUNICATIONS   Storrs, CT
May 1991   *Administrative Assistant*
Answered phones. Faxed information to media and sports
information offices. Typed and filed sports information.

Summer 1990   UCONN DEPARTMENT OF RESIDENTIAL LIFE Storrs, CT
Assistant Supervisor
Resolved problems and concerns of guests (24-hour availability).
Supervised housing facility of over 125 guests and staff of seven
Guest Liaisons. Acted as information resource for Guest Liaisons.

Guest Liaison
Assisted Conference Hall Supervisor with information processing.
Processed campus-wide routine and emergency maintenance calls.

COMPUTER   DOS, WordPerfect, Microsoft Word, Lotus 1-2-3, and
dBASE III Plus.

INTERESTS   Sailing, swimming, aerobics, piano, and ice skating.

Jonathan Simms
11 Sutton Place
Bloomfield, CT 06002
(203) 555-3145

OBJECTIVE: To use proven skills in marketing and proposal development to promote products and services for a large engineering company.

BACKGROUND: International Sales Experience
Marketing/Promotion
Budget/Forecast Preparation
Advanced Computer Skills

EDUCATION: University of Connecticut, Hartford, Connecticut
21 Credits toward M.B.A. (Marketing)
Expected Graduation — May, 1993

Yale University, New Haven, Connecticut
B.S. Mechanical Engineering — 1981

ACCOMPLISHMENTS:
Set up and managed a temporary office in Seoul, Korea, for a company negotiating team. Ensured that the staff of 4 Koreans and 2 U.S. employees met the needs of the 15 to 22 negotiators over a period of 7 months working 6 days a week, and up to 15 hours a day.

EXPERIENCE: ABB Combustion Engineering, Windsor, Connecticut

7/84–Present Nuclear Systems Business Development Specialist I

Development of customized proposals for products and services of Nuclear Systems. Sales volume responsibilities from $20 to $50 million in proposed work. Marketing, trade shows and promotional tasks for the department. Monthly monitoring and reporting on department expenditures vs. budget targets, and bookings vs. sales targets.

11/81–7/84 Primary Systems Design, Nuclear Engineer I

Generated and evaluated technical calculations for Primary Systems design in a nuclear steam supply system. Supported and coordinated with project office. Expedited schedules for engineering tasks.

John R. Dawson
8 Lee Mansion Drive
West Simsbury, CT 06090
Phone: (203) 555-5555

OBJECTIVE
An Accounting and Auditing Internship with Coopers & Lybrand.

EDUCATION
Master of Business Administration, Accounting
The University of Connecticut, Storrs CT
Expected Completion: May 1994
Bachelor of Arts, Political Science
Baylor University, Waco TX
Graduation: May 1992

INTERNSHIP EXPERIENCE
Congresswoman Nancy L. Johnson, Fall 1989
- Researched and drafted constituent correspondence
- Attended briefings for legislative staff
- Compiled briefing binder for staff members
- Researched National Drug Control Strategy
- Wrote Thesis: *The National Drug Control Strategy*

WORK EXPERIENCE
Marshalls of Avon, Summers and Winters 1989–1992
Mystic Pizza Parlor, 1988
The Hartford Insurance Group, Summer 1987
McLean Rest Home Volunteer, 1986

ACTIVITIES
Graduate Business Association, 1992
Association of Future Accountants, 1988–1992
Eucharistic Minister, 1988–1992
Student Program for Urban Development Big Brother, 1989

COMPUTER SKILLS
Microsoft Word
WordPerfect
Lotus 1-2-3

Joanne S. Collins
15 Woodlawn Place
Hartford, Connecticut 06060
(203) 555-8855

CAREER OBJECTIVE
"IDEA" consultant offering proven expertise in marketing, sales, product management, and computer/networking technologies.

SUMMARY OF QUALIFICATIONS
A resourceful executive who offers 14 years of **bottom line results, frequent promotions and innovative ideas**, with established strengths and qualifications in the areas of:

Marketing & Sales Strategy	Presentation Creation & Delivery
Business/Product Management	Document Conception & Writing
Staff Development/Motivation	Course Design & Training

EMPLOYMENT EXPERIENCE

I.   **Marketing & Product Management Experience (1987 – Present)**

A.   As **Director of Marketing** for Safari Systems (an AT&T joint venture), created a unique notebook computer image through marketing, advertising, trade shows, public relations and promotions. Directed marketing efforts, staff development and influenced future product directions.

Accomplishments: Safari achieved unprecedented sales success by far exceeding business plan ten-fold. Best press and customer acceptance of an AT&T computer product.

B.   As **Financial Solutions District Manager** for AT&T, managed computer hardware & software products designed for financial institutions. Directed product management, marketing, critical third-party relationships and staff re-deployment.

Accomplishments: Excelled in defining products, directing business and marketing efforts. Rewarded with Safari Systems position.

C.   As **National Networking Marketing Manager** for AT&T, developed data networking strategies for LAN, FDDI, bridge, router, and gateway technologies.

Accomplishments: Helped establish the AT&T Network Users Group (NUGATT) that thrives today with over 200 corporate members.

(continued)

II.   Sales Management / Direct Sales Experience

A.   As AT&T Account Manager (1986 – 1987), handled sales team management and direct sales of computer systems to government, financial, insurance, and manufacturing customers.

Accomplishments: Managed sales strategy, key customer contacts, presentations, and large sale project management. Typical contract size between $500 thousand and $4 million.

B.   As AT&T Area Staff Manager (1984 – 1986), created and disseminated marketing information to Regional sales teams.

Accomplishments: Developed materials and taught in the Northeast Sales Training Program.

C.   As AT&T Account Executive / Industry Consultant (1982 – 1984), sold telephone systems, computers and data communications networks.

Accomplishments: Awarded "Top Sales Person" consecutive years and named "Best Account Executive" in 1984 as the top salesperson east of the Mississippi River. Selected as Area Staff Manager out of over 200 qualified candidates.

D.   As New England Telephone Account Executive (1981 – 1982), sold networked communications services to State Governments.

Accomplishments: Finished 130% of annual quota. Certified as Account Executive / Industry Consultant.

E.   As Sales Representative for the Burroughs Corporation (1978 – 1981), sold on-line banking networks, mini-computers and software applications to financial institutions.

EDUCATION

Boston College	University of Connecticut
School of Management 1974–78 Bachelors of Science	School of Business Administration 1992–93 Masters Degree in Business

PROFESSIONAL AWARDS
- Regional Vice President's Award
- Area Vice President's Award
- Branch Candidate for National Excellence Award

The Application Letter

Everyone agrees that appearance is crucial in an application letter. Some personnel directors use appearance as a sole criterion for elimination. If your letter or résumé is messy, poorly organized, unattractive or error ridden, it will be ignored.

Guidelines for a good application letter

- Use quality bond paper for both your letter and résumé and buy matching envelopes. **Never** use onion skin or erasable paper. White, cream or grey are the best choices.
- Allow ample white space. Balance your letter on the page symmetrically.
- Type each letter individually. Résumés can be mass produced but not application letters. Assure that your ribbon produces crisp print (carbon ribbon preferred if typewritten; laser printer is best).
- Do **not** use unusual type faces (script, art deco, etc.).
- Sign your name with a pen in blue or black ink.
- **PROOFREAD!** Make no mistakes.

A. But above all, **generate interest in your reader**. Open with a lead that will catch his or her attention.

Most of what you say in an application letter should be based on knowledge of the company. Perhaps you have ties with the company already. You've worked there or someone you know has worked there. Mention that. Perhaps someone has recommended that company. Say so and tell why.

- Do you have a contact you can mention?
- Have you had any unusual experience that ties in with the company's interests?

B. Keep the attention section brief. In the body of your letter, **be as specific as possible**:

- Instead of saying, "I'm a good salesperson," explain that you spent a semester at Eddie Bauer's in Stamford and you were elected company-wide winner in Professional Excellence.
- Instead of speaking about your writing skills, say that you updated the "Guide to Fresh Farm Foods" at the New York Marketing Center.

C. Refer to your résumé at strategic points, but try to put into your application letter extra material that supports your candidacy.

1. Always be positive.
2. Focus on your strengths.
3. Show confidence in yourself.
4. Don't inflate yourself with bombastic phrases and grandiose claims.
5. Toe the line between straightforward, assertive remarks and cockiness. Don't put yourself forward as a genius who will reorganize the company and save it from incompetence.
6. **Empathize with your reader.** That means **focus** on him or her. What does he or she want to hear from you? Do you feel the concerns of your future employers? Will they see you as someone who can manage others effectively, increase productivity, take risks, work hard, etc.?

D. End your letter with an action step. Request an interview. **Set dates if possible**. Follow up with a phone call.

There is no such thing as a model letter of application. Each will be different. Each will reflect the empathic meeting of a specific **you** with a specific **other** (person, job, place, etc.).

EXERCISE **17** Here are some letters to consider. After reviewing them, create an application for a specific job you want. Redo your résumé if necessary to emphasize your qualifications for this specific position.

---

56 East Congress Street
Corry, PA 16407

June 6, 1991

Mr. Nick Sim, Personnel Director
Atlantic Richfield Corporation
515 South Flower Street
Los Angeles, CA 90071

Dear Mr. Sim:

While Atlantic Richfield was negotiating an off-shore drilling contract in Shanghai last spring, I was traveling independently throughout the People's Republic of China. I obtained a realistic view of the living and working environment of Shanghai and am eager to serve America's largest oil company in China's largest industrial city.

I completed 30 credits of Chinese and worked with top Chinese executives while residing for one year in Taiwan. Having majored in East Asian Studies, I acquired an in-depth knowledge of the sociopolitical atmosphere of the area. In addition, while studying at National Taiwan University, I lived in a single room with five Chinese Students. The understanding of Chinese customs and lifestyle I gained during that year will put me in a favorable position as a corporate representative.

This understanding of the language, customs, and background of the Chinese people is supported by 27 credits of business-related courses. My experience as an English instructor to executives in Taiwan has also given me considerable skill in interpersonal relations with foreign professionals. By managing my own business for eight of my eleven working years, I have acquired the techniques of making good business decisions on a daily basis.

I am very eager to discuss my qualifications for a public relations position with you. I will call you the week of Monday, July 8 to arrange an interview at your convenience.

Sincerely,

Barbara A. Boron

23 South College Avenue
Newark, DE 19711

February 12, 1990

Mr. Lewis T. Grant
Advanced Advertising Agency
401 Heritage Trail
Granbury, TX 76048

Dear Mr. Grant:

Recently, Brian Phillips of station WKWK informed me of a public relations position that is open at Advanced Advertising. I am interested in applying for that position. I feel my experience and education in radio, writing, and photography qualify me to publicize full-time for your organization.

For the past two summers, I have conducted on-air interviews on WKWK Radio with Mr. Phillips. I was trained to interview and send reports over the telephone to area radio stations. After a few stories, I learned voice control and poise on the air. At WKWK, I also learned to operate a playback machine. In radio classes at college, I mastered the entire audio board including turntables and cart machines. As I understand it, your public relations position requires knowledge of this type of equipment.

As a writer and photographer for the Campus Review, the university student newspaper, I write news releases and feature articles as well as type and edit my stories. In addition, I photograph, develop, and print pictures for the newspaper, a result of nine years of photography training. The Campus Review has also taught me to meet weekly deadlines.

My undergraduate degree in communications from the University of Delaware emphasizes the interpersonal skills necessary in public relations. As my résumé shows, my work experience and campus activities have given me the opportunity to put these theories into practice.

Mr. Phillips spoke highly of your creative approach. I believe my portfolio shows I can contribute to Advanced Advertising's creative successes. I will call you next week to see about a convenient time for an appointment. If you wish to reach me in the meantime, my number is 555-1212.

Sincerely,

Marjorie M. Murphy

131 Sutton Place
Bloomfield, CT 06002

May 25, 1991

Mr. John Doe, Personnel Manager
ZYY Engineering Company
100 Main Street
Yourtown, US 00000

Dear Mr. Doe:

Your ad in this month's *Nuclear News* for a Marketing Engineer was of special interest to me since I will soon be completing my M.B.A. in Marketing at the University of Connecticut. While your ad asks for someone with a Marketing degree, I'm writing to find out if you'd be interested in someone who has practical experience in marketing and engineering.

As you can see from my enclosed résumé, I have practical experience in marketing, international sales and engineering. I've also worked on proposals with your company as a subcontractor for the Arizona Nuclear Power Project. At that time, I worked with Mr. Robert Zirngible for several weeks, pulling together costing data and developing the market analysis for our companies' joint proposal.

While I've had some experience with ZYY Engineering, I'd be interested to find out more about any opportunities with you. ZYY Engineering's reputation and my good working relationship with the company make this a very appealing combination to me.

I would like to discuss my qualifications in depth with you. I will call next week to arrange a convenient time to talk with you. Or you can call me at (203) 555-3145 to make alternate plans.

Sincerely,

John Smith

Enclosure: Résumé

342 Summit Avenue
West Hartford, CT 06105
September 30, 1992

Mr. John Dawes, Senior Partner
J D Consultants, Inc.
1990 O'Brien Parkway
Wexford, MA 01999

Dear Mr. Dawes:

Your firm's well-known success in assisting American companies to expand their operations into the growing European marketplace is of special interest to me. I would like very much to be part of your European market development team, and have enclosed my résumé for your consideration.

To supplement my diverse experience in American business and prepare for a career in the international arena, I am pursuing appropriate graduate training, concentrating my M.B.A. course work in international business. I have developed additional expertise concerning the European Community by seeking out relevant experience connected with "Europe 1992":

- a study for ABB-Combustion Engineering of the European Economic Community and its Single Market program;

- a graduate-level Independent Study entitled "Business in Europe: 1992 and Beyond" at Limburg University, the Netherlands;

- marketing activities for a Dublin company and for the Irish-American Partnership.

For the past few years, I have been independently studying French, and I expect to complete my Master of Business Administration in May, 1994.

Like you, I recognize the great marketing opportunities for U.S. firms that increase their presence in Europe. I would like to use my comprehensive American business experience and awareness of Europe's future direction to work with you in arranging advantageous trans-Atlantic partnerships. I will call you next week, after you have had a chance to review my qualifications, to see when you would find it convenient to meet me in person.

Sincerely,

Lorraine H. Belmont

13

P R I N C I P L E

Organize a Letter
According to Its Purpose

Forgive me for writing such a long letter; I didn't have time to write a short one.

Mark Twain

One of the most common types of business writing is the letter. We are all taught that the typical letter divides into several basic parts:

- the date
- the heading
- inside address
- the subject line
- the salutation
- the body
- the complimentary close
- and the enclosure or copy lines.

Of course, the business letter is much more complex, and even a simple letter can have many parts that answer many questions and address a variety of purposes:

To introduce	To explain	To conclude
To support	To report	To state
To respond	To name	To summarize
To answer	To amplify	To offer
To justify	To inform	

You will probably be writing many letters in your business lifetime. Some of them will convey information or describe procedures. Inevitably you will argue or report the results of your work. There will be routine letters that could be handled best by pre-written forms, "boiler-plate" that covers most situations.

Everything that's been said so far will make you a better letter writer: your command of tone, your clarity, your conciseness, your sensitivity to diction, direct address, active voice and parallelism.

But most important to letter writing, to all writing for that matter, is *the way your organization reveals the purpose of your communication.* What you say first and what you say last are important. Equally important, at least initially, is how the letter looks on the page.

Bad News Letters

There are so many types of letters that it's impossible to categorize all of them. There are responses to requests or inquiry letters, letters of complaint or "bad news" letters, orders and favorable responses, and letters that have legal implications or binding contractual language. There are reports and justifications, sales letters of all kinds, and, of course, letters of introduction.

Generally, the letter that gives us pause is the "bad news" or refused request letter, which requires tact and a strategy that attempts to maintain goodwill while rejecting a point of view or a request.

Thus far, we've been stressing clarity, brevity and precision. But *tact*, or a strategy to "soften the blow," or a letter that justifies and maintains your position may lengthen a letter.

Let's look at an example or two of letters that deal effectively with bad news or refusal. In the first two letters, notice the indirection. The reader senses the bad news, but it doesn't overwhelm him/her. In the third, the news is given directly, but softened with an appraisal of the hidden benefits.

SUBJECT: Request for Donation — The "Friends of Ann Baylor" Scholarship

I have reviewed your letter concerning the "Friends of Ann Baylor" scholarship, in memory of an ABC employee killed while employed at the Environmental Laboratory. I commend you for setting up a scholarship fund with your own donations for a student from Easton High School who majors in Ann's areas of focus at college (biology, natural sciences).

Concerning your request for a matching funds donation, I am unable to offer such a donation for this scholarship. However, ABC has a Community Services Involvement program that would be able to offer your group a $100 donation toward this scholarship.

Please contact John Blazer in the New London office and address a completed CSI grant request form to him. Your grant request form should address the background provided in your letter to me. It should indicate selection criteria used for the scholarship recipient, including the fact that the scholarship selection committee is composed of appropriate representatives from Ann's family, the Environmental Laboratory, and Easton High School. Only one person from the Environmental Laboratory should complete the application.

Best of luck in your 1990 fund raising effort and in selecting a deserving candidate for the "Friends of Ann Baylor" scholarship.

14 Saint Thomas Street
Enfield, CT 06082

March 1, 1991

Anne Jones
Director, CompuTech
11 Church Street
Banfield, CT 06082

Dear Ms. Jones:

I understand from your customer representative that you recently attempted to place an order for our SuperStrength batteries to power your new SmartMouse. Evidently in placing this order your Purchasing Department was advised that the lead times for this product did not allow you to meet your immediate production requirements. Consequently, you were forced to split your first order for this product between Panasonic and us.

I apologize for any inconvenience this situation may have caused you. However, I would also like to explain the reason for the extended lead times you were quoted.

In addition to powering your SmartMouse, the SuperStrength is used to power pressurized gas masks for children and the elderly who are unable to breathe with conventional masks. These gas masks are used widely in Israel and Saudi Arabia. With the recent hostilities in the Persian Gulf, the demand for these batteries increased dramatically in mid-January. As a result, the government ordered us to re-direct all existing inventories of the SuperStrength to the Persian Gulf.

About this time, your purchasing people were attempting to place an order with us. Consequently, in the midst of attempting to resolve our own "gulf crisis," you were quoted excessive lead times. Since that time, we have increased production on this battery and are confident that we will be able to supply all of your SuperStrength needs in the future.

Ms. Jones, you are a valued customer. Though we are always working to be responsive to the needs of our customers, events periodically arise that are beyond our control. This was one of those times. Please accept our apology and rest assured that in the future we will be able to meet your requirements. Please contact me should you have any additional questions or comments.

Sincerely,

Marley M. Richler
Independent Financial Planning Consultant
(203) 555-7687

June 1, 1991

Jim Jones
11 Apple Valley
Southington, CT 06101

Dear Jim,

I've done all I can to retrieve your $5000.00 investment in the oil and gas limited partnership you purchased in 1980. I'm sorry to say, there is nothing else to do to recoup your money.

Despite the risk, and as disappointing as this is, your original attraction to the partnership was the outstanding tax advantages it could provide. In fact, it did just that. During the first three years of the partnership, you realized 50% of your original investment in tax savings. Over the next three years, a combination of cash flow and depreciation recovered another 60% of your original purchase. In total, you have received 110% of your investment in the form of tax write-offs and cash flow.

We couldn't have predicted the nature of the tax overhauls or the poor performance in the oil patch that have made this investment a dinosaur.

However, you were level-headed about the original investment. Although no loss is a good loss, this loss represents just 1% of your total assets. It will in no way affect the success of the rest of your portfolio.

Jim, if I can answer any other questions for you regarding this partnership, or if I can be of service in any other way, please call.

Sincerely,

Marley Richler

The letter on page 82 was written to explain and apologize to a customer for the late delivery of a cost statement for a pension plan. The customer is angry. As you can see from the rewrite, it can be brief, clear and crisp with a tone that is more sincere.

Before

Mr. Vincent R. Smith
500 White Plains Road
Scarsdale, New York 10583

Dear Mr. Smith:

Mr. Jones has asked me, as head of the Defined Benefits Department, to respond to your letter of November 2, 1990.

Your concern over the late delivery of the 1990 pension costs on your various plans is quite understandable. The problems you indicate certainly do not reflect the quality of service you should be expecting from us, and I regret you had to write such a letter.

The delays you have experienced are the results of problems we encountered in converting to new data systems for our pension plans. Our new database was installed in order to maintain more complete and accurate information which is necessary to meet all of the requirements of ERISA. Unfortunately, as is true with many new systems, we are experiencing a continual series of conversion problems which have considerably delayed our work on many of our pension plans. We feel we have resolved most of the problems, but are having some difficulty making up for lost time on many pension plans that are all due at the same time.

I regret that your problems had reached the crisis stage before we fully realized the nature of your needs. Unfortunately, the process of data collection, review, coding, computer applications, costs analysis and review, and so on is a rather complex chain of events and is very difficult to accelerate at this point in time. I will, however, personally make certain that every possible priority is given to completing calculations on the plans for which you do not yet have costs.

Since federal regulations provide for a range of permissible contributions, it is likely that our work will validate the level of contributions you have determined. We would, however, appreciate receiving a description of the manner in which your costs were calculated.

In the event your calculations have produced a value outside the range of permissible plan contributions, we will be happy to assist in identifying alternative treatments of 1990 plan year pension expense that might aid in avoiding any financial penalty.

We value very much the association which we have had over the years, Mr. Smith, and I want to extend my personal apologies for the problems which we are currently experiencing. I assure you that every effort will be made to complete the remaining work as quickly as possible. The necessary steps have been taken to see that this information is provided next year on a more timely basis so that you will once again be assured of receiving the kind of service which you have a right to expect.

Sincerely,

After

Mr. Vincent R. Smith
500 White Plains Road
Scarsdale, New York 10583

Dear Mr. Smith:

I appreciate your writing us about our late delivery of costs for your pension plans. Mr. Jones has asked me, as head of the Defined Benefits Department, to respond to your letter of November 26.

You're right: you deserve better service — and you will get it. I will see to it myself.

The delay stemmed from our installing new data systems to meet all the ERISA requirements. As so often happens, the systems did not work smoothly at first; and so we lost time. While we were striving to catch up, your problem developed.

Calculating costs is, as you know, complex. We must collect data, review it, code it, process it, review our results and so on. Consequently, the calculations will still take time. You have wisely allowed for that by estimating your costs. (Could you let us know how you made your estimates?)

Here is what I will do now:

1. I will give the highest priority to calculating your remaining costs.

2. Our calculations may well show that your estimate falls within the range that federal regulations permit. But if your contributions fall outside that range, I will see to it that we help you find ways that might aid you in treating your 1990 plan-year pension expenses so as to avoid any financial penalty.

We value our years of association with you, Mr. Smith. We regret that our new systems have created this problem, and I promise you that in 1991 you will receive the service you deserve.

Sincerely,

EXERCISE **18** **Choose one of the following situations and write an appropriate letter. Remember, you want to pay close attention to your audience.**

1. You are an external consultant asked to recommend changes in Paradise Pizza Company's market strategy. The CEO wants to know what you recommend.

2. Now the marketing director of Paradise Pizza wants to know what you recommend.

3. You are in charge of complaints from customers at Northeast Utilities. Someone has just written that his power was interrupted for five hours and when it was restored, his television went on the blink. Though your company is not responsible for such damage, he thinks you should compensate him. Write a courteous reply.

14

PRINCIPLE

Find a Format and Make It Visible

We typically retain:

10% of what we READ
20% of what we HEAR
30% of what we SEE
50% of what we SEE and HEAR

Perhaps the easiest way for you to approach writing on the job is to recognize that there are many situations which we can think of as typical, repeatable, standard. These situations do not call for great originality or deep thoughts. They **do** require an understanding of the form or convention used in a particular situation.

Some examples of those situations could be:

a progress report   an analytic comparison
a job description   a hazard alert
a job procedure   a strategic plan
a problem/resolution memo   a feasibility report
an option memo   a procedure
a trip report

Many people reinvent the wheel each time they create these kinds of documents. In the event that a perfectly good model already exists, use it. Here are a few good models to follow for certain documents that you will encounter:

PROGRESS REPORT

DATE: **October 24, 1993**
TO: **John Smith**
FROM: **Lee Jones**
SUBJECT: **Monthly Progress**

January   Replaced leaking coolers, coolant-contaminated cells control solenoid valves, and the water-tank heat exchanger in Build 3.

March   Held a final performance evaluation. In 1990 Build 3 ran for 53 hours with 1 start for a total of 1663 hours and 3 starts. Shut the powerplant down to install Build 4, the new powersection with metal coolers.

April   Installed Build 4. Solved problems with invertor U.P.S. circuit and with leakage in the hydrogen inlet plenum.

May   Started an endurance run.

July   Shut down plant because of invertor circuit problems.

August   Corrected those problems and restarted the powerplant. Build 4 has accumulated 2400 hours with 6 starts to date. The longest continuous run was 1722 hours. This year we have given 19 demonstrations.

Major continuing problem: Managing acid in the powersection. Lost acid corrodes components downstream, and adding acid puts the powerplant out of service.

PROGRESS REPORT

DATE: May 24, 1990
TO: John Smith
FROM: Richard Lewis
SUBJECT: PTSC IMPLEMENTATION

This is what the Project Team has done so far to start up the new Public Telephone Service Center (PTSC):

Site:
Arranged to convert 2nd floor of former Bristol Central Office for PTSC use.

Hired Grinelli Contractors. Work started 5/20; completion expected 12/20.

Placed telecommunications equipment order with Installation Department.

STILL NEEDED: Decision from Real Estate VP regarding expansion of existing parking lot to accommodate new employee and customer volume.

Staff & Training:
Posted 14 Public Telephone Service Rep job vacancies (10 filled so far).

Requested Transfer Training to train Reps in PT rates and service options.

Sent Manager requisition to Personnel Planning Committee. Hope to promote a Field Assistant Manager into this position.

Computer Systems:
Submitted job requests to Software Development to modify affected systems (Customer Records, Billing, Installation Scheduling, Maintenance).

Issued request for bid on new interactive terminals for service reps.

Methods & Procedures:
Wrote up new flow for work between PTSC and Installation. Both departments have accepted new procedure.

Arranged for Training to include specific, updated "customer contact" scripts in transfer material.

Customers:
Requested directory to include PTSC's "800" number in next phone book and in all books thereafter.

Asked Public Relations to design bulletin about new "800" number.

JOB DESCRIPTION

TO: Terry Dawson
FROM: Pat Riley
SUBJECT: Job Description
POSITION: Securities Trader

DUTIES: To buy and sell various investment securities including stocks, bonds, options, and commercial paper. Other responsibilities include:

- maintaining a trade log
- maintaining a brokerage commission budget
- recording pertinent market data on a daily basis
- preparing a weekly written report on market activity.

NATURE OF THE JOB: Extremely fast-paced and intense during market trading hours. The trader is usually working on several trades at any given time. Almost all work is done on the telephone. The trader is constantly in contact with other traders, brokers, and outside sources of information, conducting trades and maintaining an overall picture of what the markets are doing and where they are going. Can be very stressful at times.

POSITION WITHIN THE FIRM: Trader reports directly to Chief Investment Officer. Because the firm's portfolio managers and analysts work closely with the trader, their evaluation of the trader is weighed heavily in all performance reviews.

REQUIREMENTS: Candidates must have a Bachelor's degree, preferably in finance, and some experience in the financial markets. Attention to detail, organization and the ability to work in high pressure situations are essential. Some experience with computers and programs such as Lotus 1-2-3 helpful.

COMPENSATION: Includes a competitive salary and benefits package, supplemented by an annual bonus based on individual performance and overall firm profitability.

JOB PROCEDURE

Securities Trader

1. **Receive order from portfolio manager (PM).**
   a. Double-check all details (coupon rate, dollar amount, maturity, price limit) with PM.
   b. Enter all trade details on white sell ticket. **ALWAYS** initial and time-stamp the ticket!

2. **Check market price of bond on Bridge Trading System.**
   a. If you don't know the bond's ticker symbol, do a security search by typing "LU/company name" and pressing "ENTER."
   b. Once you have the symbol, type it in and press "ENTER." Write the market price at the top of the trade ticket.

3. **Always contact at least three brokers.**
   a. Use only brokers listed in the Approved Broker Directory.
   b. Write the names of the brokers you select at the bottom of the trade ticket.

4. **Contact the brokers.**
   a. Call each broker and identify yourself and the company.
   b. Indicate that you are looking for bids on a bond and give the broker the details of the trade. **ALWAYS** have the broker read trade back to you!
   c. The broker will quote you a price that is a percentage of $1000. Thus, a price of 96.37 is $963.70 per $1000 of your order.
   d. Ask the broker how long he/she is "firm" at that price. In other words, how long is that price good? So, if the price is firm for 10 minutes and you take 11 to get back to the broker, the price is subject to change. Time is critical!

5. **Confirm the order.**
   a. Once you have all your quotes, you will pick the highest price and immediately call the broker to confirm the order.
   b. As a courtesy, call the other brokers that gave you quotes and let them know what price you traded the bond at and what the "cover" (second best price) was. You do not need to tell them what broker you did the trade with.

6. **Send copy of trade ticket to PM and to Processing Department.**

7. **Enter the details of the trade in the Trade Log.**

NOTE: This is a list of <u>basic</u> procedures that apply to every sell transaction. The real **art** of trading is in the timing of trades in relation to market, the negotiating of large or inactively traded bonds, the networking of brokers and information sources, and the handling of several orders at once. These things can't be taught but must be gained with experience.

PROBLEM / SOLUTION

TO: Kevin Neilon, District Manager

FROM: Margaret Barlowe, Supervisor

PROBLEM: Time spent talking with Sales, Service and Parts departments to obtain estimates to complete cost of sales.

SOLUTION: Only the salespeople know what additional options and accessories they have included in their sales of automobiles. Therefore, they should not only list options, but label them with information disclosing who is installing these options (internal or external). In addition, the date of installation should be included so I will know if a repair order is completed or not.

This will enable me to obtain estimates of work to be performed directly from the person responsible. I will save time that was spent trying to obtain a story on every sale with options included. In addition, the profits and commissions on sales will be recorded correctly.

The Problem

	Is	**Is Not**
What	Lack of information regarding estimates of options installed	Lack of information in other parts of car sales
Where	Sales Department	Any other department
When	Every time a car is delivered (paid for) but options aren't installed yet	Sales of cars from stock without alterations
Extent	Some estimates have been off by hundreds of dollars each	All estimates

OPTION MEMO

TO: Vice President, Retail Operations

FROM: Senior Operations Analyst

SUBJECT: Staffing Recommendation
Buttermilk Mall and Shopper's Heaven Retail Outlets

ISSUE: Which of four personnel categories should we use as sales staff in new Telephone Talk shopping mall stores?

OPTION 1 – Service Representative
OPTION 2 – Service Advisor
OPTION 3 – Operator
OPTION 4 – Sales Associate

Recommendation: I recommend **OPTION 4.** Options 1–3 are too expensive and inflexible for a retail operation despite the advantages of using personnel already on the company payroll.

OPTION 1: We could reassign Service Reps who volunteer for transfer from Business Offices to Telephone Talk stores.

<u>Advantages</u>: Service Reps already in place and familiar with products, services, prices.

<u>Disadvantages</u>:
- Union contract prevents Service Reps from working non-traditional hours (as required at malls) without new union negotiations.
- Rep wages ($11.50 – $15.90 per hour plus benefits) are way over retail scale.
- Union contract guarantees 40-hour work week plus premium pay for overtime.

We cannot compete with Telephone Shack and Gabtronics if we must pay these wages.

OPTION 2: Similarly, we could reassign Service Advisors who have become "uncomfortable" with new sales quota system in Marketing Department.

<u>Advantages</u>: Good selling skills; trained to make product and service recommendations to customers.

OPTION MEMO (page 2)

Disadvantages:
- Salaries higher than Service Reps.
- Not unionized; however, their delegation to October Task Force meeting stated emphatically "No mall hours."
- Expertise is in <u>business</u> communications equipment, not in consumer items.

OPTION 3: We could reassign surplus Operators to Telephone Talk stores and avoid layoffs.

Advantages: Operators declared "surplus" (not working but still on payroll) would be more productive. Operators are trained in customer contact.

Disadvantages:
- High wages ($10.50 – $15.00 per hour), 40-hour week, and premium pay for overtime.
- No sales or product training. No guarantee they have sales aptitude.

OPTION 4: We could hire Sales Associates (new title) to conform to retail operating requirements.

Advantages: Can be hired part-time (without fringe benefits or guaranteed hours) for going retail rate of $5.50 per hour. Can be scheduled to meet precise peak and off-peak demands of each store. Not currently covered by any union contract. We can pre-screen for sales ability.

Disadvantages: Not yet hired, trained or familiar with product line. Unions may object to new hires when we have "surplus" Operators.

Please Note: Our Training Department estimates that they can make new Sales Associates fully floor-ready with one 3-hour classroom session and another 3 hours of on-the-job coaching for each employee.

We have Training's commitment that the training package will be ready by October 18.

We can begin training as soon as Personnel hires the first class of 30 Sales Associates. We can have the new employees in place for our November 1 Grand Opening.

TRIP REPORT

TO: Bill Pilson

FROM: Gladys Knight

SUBJECT: Trip Report to Regional Conferences in Panama and Jamaica

Achievements	Questions	Suggestions
Helpful in: • clarifying guidelines • contracting mechanisms • using OBR services	How do Missions meet 10% goal given that they obligate by project agreement, with contracts awarded over several years?	Determine in FY '89 what monies have been awarded, regardless of which FY funds are obligated.
	Are our reporting mechanisms efficient?	Revise reporting process or establish mechanism just for Gray Amendment contracts.
	Are routing capability statements from firms interested in specific areas useful?	Encourage firms to use data input sheet of Taurus Int; send along with capability statement.
	Are PSCs (opposed to firms) counted in Gray Amendment category?	Need more info.
	Where do local currencies count as opposed to dollars?	Need more info.
	Are IQCs attributed to field missions?	Need more info.
	Is total procurement counted under a PSA procurement?	Count total procurement.
	How can we improve field contracting?	Establish detailed guidelines; send to field to improve use.
	Do women-owned firms have special contracting mechanisms?	Conduct survey of these firms.

TRIP REPORT

TO: President, Joint Ventures Pacific Rim

FROM: Business Development Consultants

SUBJECT: Indonesia Trip, August 5 through 27, 1991

SUMMARY: My staff and I obtained Indonesian government approval for a new plant to be opened jointly with P.T. Barata. We inspected and inventoried three potential plant sites (Jakarta, Surabaya, and Serang) and compiled a preliminary list of candidates for Managing Directors.

Meeting 1: August 8 and 9, **Jakarta**. With Timoyoto Mayagar, Minister for International trade and his cabinet.

Accomplished:
- Presented proposal and our portion of financing package.
- Fielded questions from Minister and his cabinet.
- Received and evaluated Indonesian portion of financing package.

Written approval came through when we were in Surabaya!

Now we must:
- Send formal acceptance.
- Apply for Indonesian licenses.
- Submit expatriate list to Indonesian Security.
- Get funding approved by Board of Directors.

Also important: Our formal acceptance must be accompanied by the traditional "greeting" and gift from our CEO to the Minister and his family (draft enclosed).

Meeting 2: August 15 and 16, **Jakarta**. With Nakijeko Suraya, Manager of Site 1 Physical Plant.

Accomplished:
- Toured entire plant.
- Obtained detailed specifications and drawings.
- Inspected and inventoried existing equipment.

TRIP REPORT (page 2)

Now we must:
- Have Plant Engineering evaluate the Jakarta site.
- List and cost out any necessary capital improvements.

Meeting 3:   August 17 and 18, **Surabaya**. With Koko Misurika, Assistant Managing Director, Site 2.

Accomplished:
- Toured, obtained drawings, inspected and catalogued inventory.
- Obtained local appraisal of property's value.

Now we must:
- Have Plant Engineering evaluate the site.
- Cost out necessary site improvements.

Also important: We obtained the appraisal because, **although this site has an excellent harbor location, it is very run down**. We doubt that is worth even half the asking price. We should continue to consider this facility, if we can get it inexpensively and if the Plant engineers think they can retrofit it adequately. Also, we must be careful not to offend the Indonesian owners with adverse comments about the condition of this property when we offer a sharply reduced price.

Meeting 4:   August 23 and 24, **Serang**. With Wisnoentoro Javata, Deputy Production Manager, Site 3.

Accomplished:
- Completed plant tour, inspection, inventory as at other sites.
- Received Mr. Wisnoentoro's recommendations regarding appointment of new Managing Director (he recommends himself).

Now we must:
- Have Plant Engineering evaluate the site.
- Cost out necessary capital improvements.
- Thank Mr. Wisnoentoro for his help and respond to his request for consideration as Managing Director.

My staff and I met frequently at our hotels when we were not meeting with the Indonesians. One of the products of our private sessions is the attached preliminary **list of 15 Managing Director candidates**. During our visits, we spoke at length with over 40 managers, foremen, and superintendents and found the listed people to be the most qualified.

EXERCISE **19** The memo below is going to the White House. Rewrite the memo, making it brief and clear. Be sure that the main point is clearly stated near the beginning. Remember how busy the White House is with thousands of communications coming in.

TO:　　　Janet Peckinpaugh
FROM:　　Don Zimmer
SUBJECT: AIRPORT CONSTRUCTION IN GRENADA

This is in reference to our telephone conversation today.

On 2 November 1983, Mr. John Sanford, Congressional Research Services, requested (on behalf of a Representative of the House who serves on the Foreign Relations Committee — Democrat) information pertaining to the involvement of AID in the construction of the airport in Grenada, prior to 1979.

After thoroughly researching the question, I provided Mr. Sanford with the following information:

In 1966, a study was commissioned by the USA, Canada, and the U.K. to make an economic survey of the English-speaking Caribbean islands, including Grenada. That study recommended the establishment of a regional development bank for the territories.

A subsequent UEDP team more fully developed the proposal and recommended, in July 1967, the establishment of the Caribbean Development Bank (CDE). The CDE was formally established in January 1970.

Originally, $20 million was targeted for the Special Development Fund of the DCE. The breakdown of contributions is as follows: USA — $10 million, UK — $5 million, Canada — $5 million. These funds were to be committed by 1973, when a review of the funding arrangements was to be done.

In 1972, the Grenada government borrowed $50,400 from CDE for an airport extension at Pearl. These funds came from the USA, Canada and the U.K.

In 1973, an AID loan was made to DCE for the construction of the Carriacou airport ($50,000).

For the period of August 1973 – December 1975, $200,000 from the USA, Canada and the U.K. were allocated to the CDE for tourism in Grenada (this includes many projects such as the construction of hotels).

In 1976, the World Bank, the USA, Canada and the U.K. were studying the possibility of conducting a Feasibility Study on the construction of the airport at Pearl. The problems that were cited include the lack of night lights for landing and the length of the runway. The construction at Pearl was deemed not to be cost effective and attention was turned to the possibility of a Feasibility Study at Point Salinas.

The World Bank wanted to conduct the Feasibility Study. The Grenadans argued that the USA, U.K. and Canada should bear the costs of the Feasibility Study which were estimated at $2 million. The project itself would have cost $40 million.

Canada was willing to aid Grenada in the costs. The U.K. later indicated the willingness to construct the control tower and install the landing lights.

The Feasibility Study never did take place because the Cubans were willing to undertake the project by constructing a 9,000-foot runway at Point Salinas without a Feasibility Study.

15

PRINCIPLE

Use a Visual Layout to Help the Eye of the Reader

What the eye doesn't catch, the mind grieves after.

Jacques Barzun

As we've examined formats of documents you will write, you must have been struck by the degree to which you were able to see instantly what the writer wished to convey. Your job as a writer is to get your views across:

- **Clearly:** You want your readers to grasp exactly what you mean.
- **Briefly:** You want to please your readers by saving their time and energy.
- **Persuasively:** You want to make your ideas stick.

You have seen how your tone of voice, your choice of words, and your understanding of audience can make a difference. But even after you've mastered all that, you won't be a powerful writer unless you use principles of **visual layout**.

As you plan what you are going to write and as you write, ask yourself, **"How can I lay this material out so that my reader can see quickly, easily, and precisely what is important to him or her? Are there paths for the reader? Can the reader scan the document and find meaning quickly?"** Below are some of the devices you can use. However, don't use too many devices at one time. Overused, they can become "noise."

For **typed texts** you can draw on:

- Spacing
- Capitalizing
- Underlining
- Numbers
- Letters

For **printed texts** you can draw not only on those five devices but also on typefaces, colors and other design devices.

You can use the following for a variety of layouts:

1. Paragraphs
2. Sections
3. Headings
4. Graphs
5. Tables
6. Problem/solution formats
7. Flow charts
8. Representational drawings
9. Lists, outlines, check-offs
10. Computer graphic designs

In the following example, the original memo, with its large chunks of prose, is visually unappealing. The length of the line is too long, and the reader can't scan it easily. The possibility of anyone reading it is negligible. In the "after," one can see meaning immediately, at a glance. The use of a comparative analysis in tabular form, the breakout of statistics, the isolation of a note and the (a) and (b) of the conclusion allow the reader to take in the information in comfortable chunks.

Before

Wire Transfer of Funds:

One of the Controller's 1988 Action Plans calls for analyzing the present policy for wire transfer of funds from regional boxes to Hartford and comparing this system with alternatives to determine the best overall method. In this regard, Mike and John, both representatives of Hartford National, had a meeting with us this morning. Also present at the meeting were Skip and Lin. The following summarizes what John and Mike discussed with us.

Basically, there are two methods of transferring the funds from lock box to Hartford. One is the wire transfer method, the one that we currently use. The other is the depository transfer method. Under this method the funds are electronically transferred from a lock box to Hartford. Under both the methods, the funds are made available the following day. Under the wire transfer method, the transferrer bank wires funds to the transferee bank, in this case Hartford National, on a daily basis. The funds transferred today are available for use tomorrow. Under depository transfer method, the transferrer bank informs an independent agent of the day's deposit. The independent agent, usually a data corporation, immediately stores the information in a computer tape. The funds stored in this computer tape are transferred by this independent agent to the transferee bank—Hartford National the same day. The Hartford National Computer Center will process the data the same day and the funds will be credited to the customer's account — Aetna's account, on the same day. To take a concrete example, let us assume that the bank in Atlanta informs the independent agent the day's deposit by 2:00 p.m. Eastern time. By 6:00 p.m., when the independent agent has produced a master tape of all transactions of all the banks within their geographic location, the tape is given to Hartford National By 9:00 p.m. the Hartford National Computer Center would have processed the deposits (computer tape) and credited Aetna's account. Aetna is, thus, in a position to use a substantial portion of these deposits for its use the following day. In terms of availability thus, both methods would appear identical.

Given the same availability advantage, it appears that the depository transfer method would offer substantial savings in the cost of transferring funds. Whereas it costs $6 per deposit transfer under wire transfer method, it would cost less than $1 under depository transfer method. Presently there are nine transfers a day for the present nine banks. Assuming that there are approximately 250 working days in the year, it costs us about $13,500 annually to use the wire transfer method. On the basis of $1 a day for each of the nine banks, it would cost us approximately $2,250 annually. Annual savings of about $11,250 appears probable. Mike and John have given us to understand that there are no other "set up" costs associated with depository transfer method system.

If we decide to make a switch to this alternative, the points to consider are whether we would like to use the services of an independent agent, or deal directly with Hartford National Bank. It is possible not to use the services of an independent agent if we could provide Hartford National with "deposits" in a computer tape form as an independent agent would do. Since there is a heavy demand on our computer capabilities, it may not seem possible to deal directly with the bank. Among the independent agents the two most prominent are NBC and Rapid Data, Inc. Rapid Data employs electronic voice to record the information from the transferrer bank. This requires that the transferrer bank has touch-tone capabilities. NBC uses operators after inputting the information into the system, can read it back to the caller. It should be noted though that since NBC is a leader in this field, they are overloaded with volume and could present some delays occasionally. It takes approximately 3 to 4 weeks for the system to be functional. Hartford National will begin the process should we decide to proceed and make a switch.

After

WIRE TRANSFER OF FUNDS

PROJECT: Analyze the present policy for wire transfer of funds from regional boxes to Hartford and compare this system with alternatives to determine the best overall method. The alternative to Wire Transfer is the Depository Transfer Check (DTC) method.

COMPARATIVE ANALYSIS:

	Wire Transfer	**Depository Transfer**
Mechanics of Transfers	The bank receiving the funds wires them to HNB.	The bank receiving the funds wires information about collected funds to HNB through an independent agent.
Availability Factor	We have access to the funds the following day except for Trust Co. of Georgia that has same-day availability.	We have access to funds the following day for all banks, including Trust Co. of Georgia.
Ease, convenience & efficiency	It is an easy, convenient and efficient system.	It is more efficient & more reliable than wire transfer.
Annual Cost:		
a. Number of daily transactions	9	9
b. Number of work days/year	250	250
c. Total yearly transactions	2,250	2,250
d. Cost per yearly transaction	$6.00	$1.00
e. Total annual cost	$13,500.00	$2,250.00

Note: Under DTC method, the Trust Co. of Georgia funds will be available after 24 hours. The average daily funds transferred from Trust Co. of Georgia are $115,000. The loss of interest income, assuming there are 250 work days in a year, would be $37.00. Since the amount is not material it has not been considered in above computation of cost.

CONCLUSION: I conclude that a switch to DTC is desirable.

a. It offers the same advantages as wire transfer.

b. It will result in cost savings of about $11,250.

There are non "set-up" costs associated with the switch and Hartford National Bank can make the system operational in about four (4) weeks.

Among independent agents, NBC and Rapid Data Inc., are prominent. Rapid Data uses computer "voice" to record deposits and requires touch-tone capabilities. NBC uses "live" operators and is preferable.

Curb Your Tendency to Start with Background Information!

Poor writing can be dangerous to your health! The following General Services Administration Bulletin was attached to the walls of GSA buildings in Washington, DC. It was supposed to warn employees who work around pigeon habitations about the dangers of pigeon droppings.

By the time the workers could read the original memo, they would have inhaled the fungus or been covered with droppings. In the rewrite, there is some hope. But the **best** way would have been to put up a sign: **DON'T TOUCH!**

Before

79-3	POTENTIAL BIOLOGICAL HAZARD	March

Background: During evaluations in a historic older building that GSA proposes to restore, a large accumulation of pigeon droppings was discovered that had collected through long habituation of the birds. Samples of the droppings were collected and analyzed by the Center for Disease Control in Atlanta, Georgia.

Discussion: The Center identified the droppings as containing a fungus capable of causing very serious infections in humans. This fungus is called "Cryptococcus Neoformans". It attacks lungs, the central nervous system, skin, eyes, liver and joints, and has a marked target of the brain and meninges. It is contained in the accumulation of excretion of birds and pigeons in old nesting areas, and in soil contaminated with bird and pigeon droppings.

Workers who work around or demolish bird and especially pigeon habitations should use extreme caution due to the potential risk of illness involved when disturbing accumulations prior to decontamination. Infection is primarily due to inhalation. Prevention is possible by wearing appropriate face masks and personal protective clothing.

Recommendation: If such an area is identified, do not disturb it, leave the area, and report the finding immediately to your supervisor. Supervisors will coordinate with Regional Accident and Fire Prevention Branches for evaluation, preventive measures, and decontamination action.

Further information: Avoid suspected area until it has been determined not hazardous.

Regional Accident and Fire Prevention Branches have information concerning this disease and decontamination requirements. Contact Roy Ashley, FTS. 566-0961

After

HAZARD: PIGEON (AND OTHER BIRD) DROPPINGS

WHO IS AFFECTED?

Those who work around or demolish pigeon (or other bird) habitats.

WHAT IS THE DANGER?

A fungus capable of causing very serious infections in humans.

The fungus is called "Cryptococcus Neoformans". It attacks lungs, the central nervous system, as well as skin, eyes, liver and joints, and has a marked target of the brain and meninges.

The fungus is contained in the accumulation of bird excretion in old nesting areas, and in soil contaminated with bird droppings.

RECOMMENDATION: If you identify an area with an accumulation of bird droppings:

1. <u>Don't touch it</u>
2. <u>Leave the area</u>
3. <u>Report it to your supervisor</u>
4. <u>Avoid the area until it is safe</u>

FOR FURTHER INFORMATION: Contact Roy Ashley 566-0961

Regional Accident and Fire Prevention Branches have information provided by the Center for Disease Control on the characteristics of this disease and the methods for decontaminating an area.

BACKGROUND:

During evaluations in an historic building that GSA proposes to restore, a large accumulation of pigeon droppings was discovered. Samples of the droppings were collected and analyzed by the Center for Disease Control, in Atlanta, Georgia. The Center identified the droppings as containing a fungus capable of causing serious infections in humans. Infection is contracted primarily through inhalation. It is possible to prevent infection by wearing appropriate face masks and personal protective clothing.

The following samples show how a visual format applies to letters as well as memos.

BEFORE

Mr. Joseph W. Saranko
Lithia, FL 33547

Dear Mr. Saranko:

This is in reply to your letter requesting information on importing dried insect specimens, seeds, plants, a live macaw, and an iguana into the United States from South America.

The importation of plant propagative material is governed by the provisions of the Nursery Stock, Plants, Roots, Bulbs, Seeds and Other Plant Products Regulations. These regulations are necessary to prevent entry of unwanted plant pests into the United States. A copy of 7 CFR 319.37 is enclosed. Section 319.37-2 lists those materials that are prohibited entry.

A permit is required for the entry of plant propagative materials. We enclose two copies of PPQ Form 587, Application for Permit. Permits may be obtained without charge by completing and forwarding one copy to the Hyattsville, Maryland, address at the bottom of the form. The permit will specify the ports of entry authorized.

All plant propagative material is subject to inspection on arrival and to treatment if inspection findings warrant. Small shipments can usually be cleared within 24 hours. However, shipments arriving at the end of the week may be held over till the next week for clearance. All shipments should be planned to enter at Nogales, Ariz.; Los Angeles, San Diego, or San Francisco, Calif.; Miami, Fla.; Honolulu, Hi.; New Orleans, La.; New York, N.Y. (including J.F. Kennedy Airport); San Juan, P.R.; Brownsville, El Paso, or Laredo, Tex.; or Seattle, Wash., where special inspection facilities are available.

Plant propagative material must be accompanied by a phytosanitary certificate from the plant protection service of country of origin. (If the country of origin does not maintain a system of inspection for determining plant material is free of plant pests, the certificate does not apply.)

All orchid, cycad, and cactus plants, and many other kinds of plants are subject to the Endangered Species Convention Regulations. You may wish to contact the Wildlife Permit Office, Fish and Wildlife Service, U.S. Department of the Interior, Washington, DC 20240, for further information. If you apply for an import permit on PPQ Form 587, additional information on these regulations will be sent to you with the quarantine permit. A permit is not required for the importation of dead insect specimens. However, they are subject to inspection on arrival at the port of entry.

After

Dear Mr. Saranko:

This is in reply to your request for information on importing dried insect specimens, seeds and plants, a live macaw parrot, and an iguana.

<u>Seeds</u>: There are three requirements for importing seeds (or other plant propagative material) into the United States:

1. <u>A permit</u>. You can get a permit without charge by completing one copy of PPQ Form 587, and sending it to the Hyattsville, MD, address at the bottom of the form (we enclose 2 copies of the form). The permit will specify the authorized ports of entry.

2. <u>Inspection of seeds when they arrive</u> (and treatment if inspection findings warrant). Small shipments can usually be cleared within 24 hours. However, shipments arriving at the end of the week may be held over until the next week for clearance. You should plan your shipments to enter where special inspection facilities are available at: Nogales, AZ; Los Angeles, CA; San Diego, CA; San Francisco, CA; Miami, FL; Honolulu, HI; New Orleans, LA; New York, NY (including JFK Airport); San Juan, PR; Brownsville, TX; El Paso, TX; Laredo, TX; Seattle, WA.

3. <u>A phytosanitary certificate</u> from the plant protection service of country of origin. This **must** accompany the seeds. This does not apply if the country of origin does not have a system of inspection for determining that plant material is free of pests.

AUTHORITY FOR THESE REQUIREMENTS: The Nursery Stock, Plants, Roots, Bulbs, Seeds and Other Plant Products Regulations. These regulations are necessary to prevent the entry of unwanted plant pests into the United States. I enclose a copy of 7 CFR 319.37. Section 319.37-2 lists materials that are prohibited.

<u>Plants</u>: All orchid, cycad and cactus plants, and many other kinds of plants, are subject to the Endangered Species Convention Regulations. You may wish to contact the Wildlife Permit Office, Fish and Wildlife Service, U.S. Department of the Interior, Washington, DC 20240, for further information. If you apply for an import permit on PPQ Form 587, you will receive additional information on these regulations with the quarantine permit.

<u>Dead Insect Specimens</u>: You don't need a permit for these, but they must be inspected when they arrive at the port of entry.

<u>Parrot and Iguana</u>: We are forwarding your letter to the Veterinary Services of this Department. They will send you information on importing live animals.

Help the Eye of the Reader with Computer Graphics

With the proliferation of computers in today's business environment, it has become increasingly easy to add visual emphasis to your writing. Regardless of the type of computer you use, there are literally dozens of first-rate graphics packages available.

These packages make a simple task of inserting graphs, charts, symbols, fonts, or bullets into business documents. The added emphasis of explanatory graphics can help make your point in a concise and dramatic fashion. The information is summarized visually and requires little explanation. However, graphics should not be used to decorate a page; they should be used to make information clearer.

Before you use a graphic, you should determine its purpose. What do you want your readers to understand? Do you want them to see a performance comparison in a given time period? Do you want them to take note of a trend over time? Once you decide what you want the reader to see, you can decide the clearest way to show it.

Figure 15-1

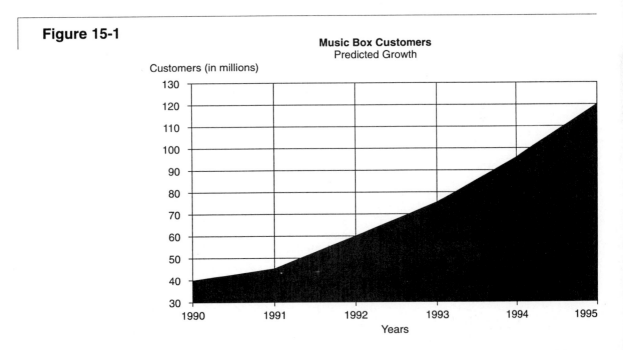

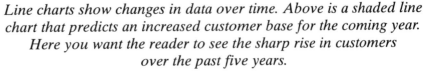

Line charts show changes in data over time. Above is a shaded line chart that predicts an increased customer base for the coming year. Here you want the reader to see the sharp rise in customers over the past five years.

105

Figure 15-2

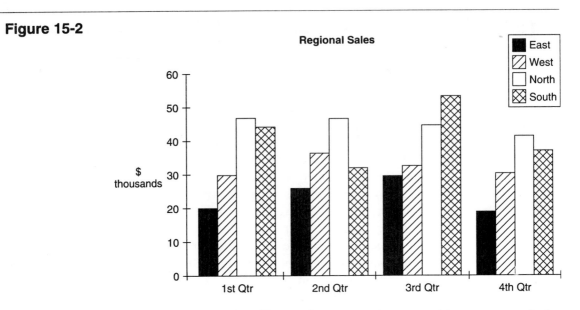

Bar charts are most effective for comparing quantities over a period of time. This chart compares quarterly sales figures for various regions of the country.

Figure 15-3

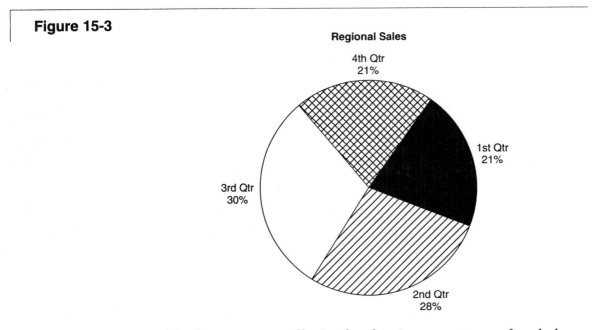

Pie charts are most effective for showing percentages of a whole. This chart shows relative sales percentages for each quarter.

Figure 15-4

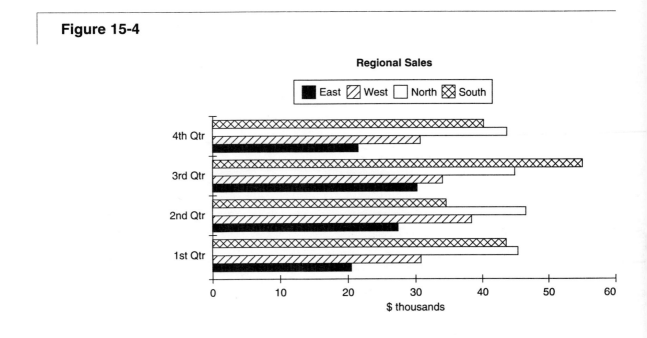

Figure 15-5

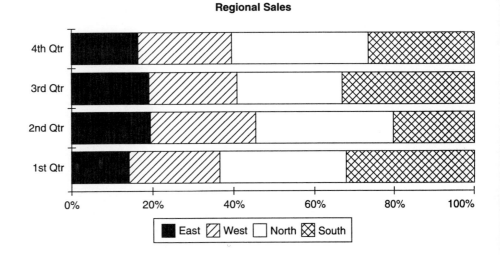

Both of these bar charts show changing relationships.
Figure 15-4 compares gross dollar sales, while Figure 15-5
shows the change in relative percentage of sales.

Figure 15-6

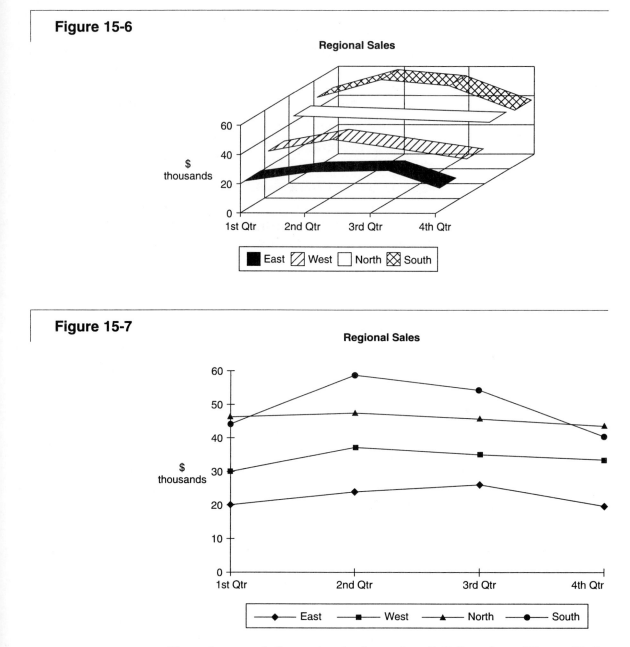

Here, the same information is shown in a 3-D line chart (Figure 15-6) and a 2-D line chart (Figure 15-7). They both demonstrate changes over time as well as data comparison. The bottom one is clearer and more precise because it isn't slanted or distorted for 3-D effect. Remember, graphics should be used to make information clearer.

Table Formats

It is often surprising how much information can be condensed in table formats. Project status reports, auditing reports, and even minutes can benefit from this kind of creative documentation. Although traditional companies still cling to the **"low-impact"** style of unbroken, chunky paragraphs, those companies that want to save reader time (which really **is** money) use streamlined **"high-impact"** documents.

A study by James Suchan and Robert Colucci done for the Naval Postgraduate School in Monterey, California, indicated that the high-impact style would save the Navy from $17.5 to $55 million annually by eliminating wasteful reading and re-reading of dense documents.

Examine the following documents to see how the high-impact style helps the reader get the necessary information at a glance.

AUDIT REPORT

Topic	Date	Deficiency	Action
$150 check from HCM	1/10/89	Check was not posted to transmittal sheet	Check must be posted on transmittal sheet
Receipt issued for $64.88 for a $50.00 check	2/7/89	$14.88 was listed as cash payment instead of $64.88	Transmittal should reflect both amounts
Receipt #108853	3/2/89	Address and total were missing	Complete receipts in full
Ten postdated premium checks totalling $1,067.41	Checks dated from 3/16 to 3/30 1989	a. Checks dated 10 days after due-date b. Checks dated less than 10 days after due-date	a. Send check back with terse memo b. Send check to Peterboro

The following format can save lots of time. Meetings are shortened when people know the focus is on *action*.

MINUTES

Human resources sector council minutes of June 28, 1989

Issue	Action	Speaker	Comment
S&T Associates	None	Zagorin	S&T Committee made up of Ayers, Parsons, Smith and Nicholson.
		Nicholson	Housing Office is interested in becoming Associates. Problem is that position descriptions don't reflect technical requirements of job.
		Heyman	What about work in general technology and science? Also, aren't financial analysts technicians?
		Zagorin	Issues like these should be brought before the designations committee and then the council if necessary. Paper has procedures for disputes.
		Barlowe	What if you don't want to be a member?
		Nicholson	Membership not voluntary.
Communication with the Field	Issue will be put on agenda when mailing list is developed.	Zagorin	What material would be helpful to send to field missions?
		Barlowe	Summary but not actual minutes.
		Nicholson	Minutes without names?
		Kline	No, because field people should know what their regional bureau representatives are saying.
		Heyman	Prefer sending important material himself, not through the council.

EXERCISE **20** Rewrite the following memo in a table format. You should use column headings to clarify the information (for example: NAME, RATING, REASONS, REMARKS, or something similar).

TO: Jack Carter
FROM: Wendy Phillips
SUBJECT: Employees with Performance Ratings below "Fully Meets Expectations"

This is in response to your memo dated November 21, 1989.

The following is the status of Central Region's employees who fail to meet performance expectations.

Bill was hurt and had been on light duty for a period of time. When his light duty status was lifted in April, he indicated to his supervision he did not want to do line work anymore. Supervision subsequently put him on the pole truck and suspended his TMP training. His absenteeism also deteriorated over the summer; consequently, he was put on no-work no-pay. At this time, Bill is still on the classification. His performance rating, therefore, is still an 002. He is looking for another position in the Company, but, due to attendance and performance, is having trouble securing a position.

Due to the suspension of his TMP training, Bill is not in a formal Performance Improvement Program at this time.

Ratings:	002 2/1/89	003 7/6/87
	002 7/16/88	002 7/6/86

Mary's performance is an 002. Mary is in a Performance Improvement Program but does not consistently maintain a Fully Meets Expectations. Her performance, therefore, is still an 002. Her prior ratings have been 003.

Dan's 002 rating is solely due to poor attendance. His attendance problems stem from war injuries and the nature of work he is currently doing. He is, however, a very competent worker when he is here. He is currently on a no-work no-pay status and his attendance has improved.

Ratings:	002 2/1/89	002 2/1/88

16

PRINCIPLE

Organize Your Thinking by Choosing the Best Structure for Your Reader

Start writing by thinking, not wrestling with words.

Jonathan Price

A "structure" is analogous to the foundation and frame of a house, or a bridge, or a ship, or the human skeleton. It's important to make your structures **visible** to your readers. There are a number of graphic models that provide a visual representation of facts and concepts and their relationships within an organized frame. They have proven to be effective tools for:

- representing abstract information in concrete form
- depicting relationships among facts and concepts
- organizing and elaborating ideas
- relating new information with prior knowledge
- storing and retrieving information effectively.

You can use these graphic structures as templates in many situations. Remember, avoid reinventing the wheel in **every** business situation.

The following is a good structure for planning an argument.

PROBLEM	GOAL(S)

ALTERNATIVES	PROS (+) & CONS (−)
	(+)
	(−)
	(+)
	(−)

DECISION(S)	REASON(S)

I. This is a good flow chart for depicting business plans.

SEQUENCE CHAIN FOR [   ]

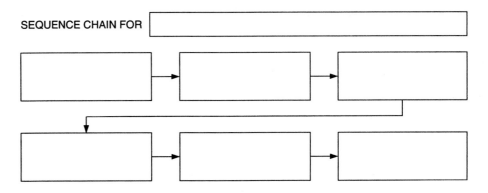

II. Engineers often use this type of format for oral presentations.

Volume: _____   Name: _____

Section: _____   Phone: _____

TOPIC: _____

Thesis Sentence (Write Last — Summarize Theme Body)

Start Here (State Point of Each ¶)
1.

2.

3.

Title: _____

4.

Caption: _____

Your CEO may require a company-wide format for certain situations. For example, on the next page is a format preferred by the CEO of a large company. Because he is inundated with proposals and reports that require decisions, he prefers overviews and a disciplined brevity.

PREPARING A LANDSCAPE SUMMARY

WHY   Writing a landscape summary does three important things.
- It forces you to focus on your most important points.
- It helps uncover gaps in your thinking.
- It provides management with a "big-picture" snapshot of critical decision-making information.

WHAT   A landscape summary should present your main observation and supporting facts in a clear, concise form. At our firm, a summary is *typically:*
- one page
- turned sideways (landscape)
- divided into boxes to separate different kinds of information

There are no strict formats. You must decide what is most important. How you structure your information will be determined by *what* you're saying and to *whom* you're saying it.

HOW   First, do rigorous research and analysis as you normally would. Landscape summaries come afterward; they don't replace the analytical process.

Second, focus on what you would say if you had only a few minutes to present your information.

Third, use *whatever best makes your point.* That may include text, tables, options, charts, matrices, graphs, flow charts or references to other documents.

WHEN   Landscape summaries should primarily be used to present information to decision makers. You may also find them helpful in other ways.

HINTS   *Be concise.* Don't try to fill up the whole page. Make sure your thoughts are complete, but compact.

Be specific. Use real numbers, estimates or ranges rather than vague amounts.

Be practical. Pursue the spirit of a summary rather than a rigid rule. If necessary, attach a larger document.

The following memo uses a visual structure to condense a great deal of information.

TO: Elizabeth Jones
FROM: Dan Zacharias
SUBJECT: <u>WESTERN</u> <u>REGION</u> <u>ACCOUNT</u> <u>VISIT</u>

This is a summary of my recent account visit with the Western Region Field Sales Office. I have included some miscellaneous items for consideration by our customers and field people.

<u>BURATA INC.</u> — **Cellular Phones**

        ATTENDEES: Ernest Downing (Director of Marketing)

        OBJECTIVE: Discuss concept of Primary Batteries for Cellular Phones.

        RESULTS: Burata is very interested in pursuing a primary battery option for their Cellular Phones. Burata-USA is an autonomous business unit of Burata, Int'l. This will allow them to retain control of this product development.

        ACTION: 1. Ernest will send electrical specs to Cheryl Price by 5/15.
                  2. Evercell will provide concept drawings of service life by 6/1.

<u>FUJIMOTO INC.</u> — **Cellular Phones**

        ATTENDEES: Amos Burns (Project Leader), George Banth (Sales Manager)

        OBJECTIVE: Discuss progress of Cellular Phone Project and determine next steps.

        RESULTS: Amos is still waiting for quotes from two vendors. He expects to receive these by 5/1, and expects to begin production within 30 days of receiving all quotes.

                  George will include five Evercell AA's with the product, and the product packaging will make reference to the Evercell Batteries Included.

        ACTION: 1. Provide George with AA Line Art by 5/15.
                  2. Prepare and present Batteries Included materials by 5/15.

EXERCISE **21** Design a visual structure for a report. Decide whether you're persuading or just giving information. Some possibilities are: business plans, sales reports, quality control reports, personnel requirements, feasibility studies, operating reports, etc.

Choose topic headings and create an outline using an alphanumeric system, logic tree or mind map. Imagine the questions your readers might raise. Your topic headings should address those questions in the order that is best for the reader. Look at the structure of the following audit report as a good example.

AUDIT REPORT: MATERIALS HELD BY VENDORS

In conjunction with our regular audit of XYZ Division, we have performed a comprehensive review of Materials Held by Vendors (MHV). As of December, XYZ Division had $125 million of MHV at 325 vendors across the United States and Canada. Our review focused on operating procedures, internal accounting controls and computerized data systems supporting the accounting for this inventory.

Summary of Findings

Our review identified several opportunities that should help division personnel to manage and control MHV inventory more effectively:

1. Procedures for communicating the availability of surplus and residual MHV inventory to procurement personnel are not adequate.

2. Financial reserves have not been established for excess and obsolete inventory as required by XYZ financial policies.

3. Several significant purchase orders require manual review and adjustment to redistribute credit balances to appropriate manufacturing orders.

4. Inventory records have not been reconciled to the general ledger since September.

5. Account reconciliation procedures do not comply with XYZ Financial policy.

6. Segregation of MHV accounting duties is inadequate, accounting records are inadequately controlled and documentation of supervisory review and approval is insufficient.

The rest of this report details the six findings above.

The following outline is the skeleton of a long-term strategy document to be used to educate three business units within a large corporation. The document will be sent to all Human Resource, Finance and Information Systems departments throughout the corporation.

EMPLOYEE SYSTEM SERVICES CONSOLIDATION PROJECT

1. Introduction
  1.1 Executive Summary
  1.2 History of ESS's Long-Term Strategy Development
  1.3 Project Methodology
      1.3.1 Developing familiarity of United Technologies Corporation
      1.3.2 Library and Publication Research

2. The ESS Long-Term Strategy Foundation
  2.1 Guidelines for the Design
  2.2 Foundation for the Strategic ESS Plan
      2.2.1 Human Resources Issues
      2.2.2 Human Resources Managers
      2.2.3 ESS Support
          2.2.3a Employee System Consolidation Project
          2.2.3b Maintaining Functional Specifications
      2.2.4 Technological Advancements
  2.3 Foundation Caveats

3. Strategic ESS Plans
  3.1 Training of System Owners
      3.1.1 Strategy of the ESS System
      3.1.2 OFI Awareness
  3.2 Proving the System
      3.2.1 Pre-Implementation Benchmarking
      3.2.2 ESS Implementation Case Study
  3.3 Adding Continuous Improvement to the System

4. Conclusions and Recommendations
  4.1 The Current Status of ESS
  4.2 Closing the Gap between Strategy and Practice
  4.3 The ESS System as a Competitive Advantage for UTC

17

Structure Your Reports According to Function

Form follows function.

Frank Lloyd Wright

In writing a report, you must first determine its function. What are you trying to accomplish? The principle of design which applies is that the form of your report follows its function.

Just as in letter and memo writing, the purpose is paramount. Next comes audience. What do they need to know first, second, third, etc. There is an infinite variety of forms; because business situations differ, reports will vary in length, format, tone, types of evidence, etc. You will analyze some of them in this chapter. Just remember the underlying principle rather than the individual forms you'll be examining.

If you are solving a problem, the solution will be shaped by the way you define the problem. Problems have many causes. If you define the problem as **motivation**, you will have to concentrate on a solution of incentives. If the problem is **misunderstandings**, you might have to hire specialists in cultural diversity in the workplace or a consultant on styles of communication. If the problem is one of **downsizing**, you will bypass incentives and understanding and focus on cost containment.

If the report involves recommendations, it is an argument and you should:

1. Define the claim or claims
2. Support with sufficient evidence
3. Determine your rationale(s)

This structure is discussed in detail in Principle 18 on rational argument.

If the report is not an argument (i.e., does not have recommendations that are claims), you will organize the information according to the reader's needs. Always define the claim or purpose on the first page and give the reader a structure or roadmap to follow.

Another approach is a structure highlighting the questions that need to be answered. In fact, your topic headings can be those questions. Remember what we've said about writing for the reader, not for yourself. Consider how the document will be used. Will it go to multiple audiences? How much background information is needed for your primary audience? Can you put some of the background into an appendix? Should you be formal or informal in tone? Will the people who read your report need a quick turn-around? Or is this the kind of report that will float from department to department or out to a broader audience? How detailed must it be? Can it be a brief report that states what should be done, its costs, and a recommended vendor?

If it is a full formal report, it requires the following additional forms:

- transmittal letter
- title page
- table of contents
- table of models
- executive summary
- body of report
- appendices

If it is not such a report, it could use other kinds of organizational structures. Using three principles of organization, the argument structure could be:

1. comparison/contrast
2. problem/solution
3. option

All of these would involve recommendations or claims. The topic headings might be:

1. Statement of Problem
   Background Information

Analysis
Proposed Solution

2. Statement of Purpose
Question: Should we do A, B or C?
Recommendation: We should do C, because...

3. Statement of Problem
Statement of Advantages/Disadvantages
Discussion of A, B and C
Recommendation/Conclusion

You can choose to leave out the advantages of the options you don't want if they are impractical or too costly or farfetched. Remember, if you are presenting information without recommendation, you simply need to organize according to some pattern that serves the reader's interests — general to specific, chronological, psychological, etc.

Winston Churchill sent the following message to his war cabinet during World War II. It contains the essence of what we've been saying about excellent writing throughout this text:

> To do our work, we all have to read a mass of papers. Nearly all of them are far too long. This wastes time while energy is spent looking for essential points. I ask my colleagues and their staffs to see to it that their reports are shorter.
>
> 1. The aim should be reports which set out the main points in a series of short, crisp paragraphs.
> 2. If a report relies on detailed analysis of some complicated factors, or on statistics, these should be set out in an appendix.
> 3. Let us have an end to...wooly phrases that are mere padding, which can be left out altogether or replaced with a single word. Let us not shrink from using the short expressive phrase, even if it is conversational.[4]

Executive Summaries

If your report is longer than five pages, you should include a one-page executive summary that covers the important points. If you've ever written an abstract of an article or dissertation, you know how hard it is to condense all you've written into a brief description.

4 Winston Churchill, Public Record Office, August 1940. Quoted from D.W. Erving, *Writing for Results in Business, Government and the Professions* (New York, 1974). Today, I would add **"Particularly** if it is conversational."

But this concept of an executive summary serves the reader well. It is written primarily for busy executives who have little time to read the whole report.

Follow the structure of your report, selecting the essential, including facts and figures, conclusions and recommendations. If you've followed a Claim, Evidence, Rationale structure, the executive summary will be easier to write. Conclusions and recommendations will appear at the beginning. Introductory material and evidence will follow.

NOTE: Database searches currently retrieve information by keying on the first 100 words in a document. This should encourage you to use a C, E, R structure.

E X E R C I S E **22** Examine the following models of Executive Summaries. Now write a summary of your own report. Remember, the important information should be condensed onto one page and placed in a clear visual format. Make the information readily accessible to the eye of the reader.

MODEL #1: EXECUTIVE SUMMARY

Statement of Problem: Two problems initiated our review of Strong-Standard's health insurance program: increasingly high premiums and slow claim payment processing.

Rationale: Blue Cross/Blue Shield has not provided a solution. We asked three other insurance companies and two health maintenance organizations (HMO's) to provide quotes. When we saw they couldn't come up with solutions, we decided to investigate self-insurance.

Solution: We have concluded that self-insurance is the answer using SafeCo as a third-party administrator (TPA).

Evidence: The advantages are:

1. Only a 10% increase because of a less expensive TPA
2. A promise that claims will be processed in 2 weeks
3. Reduced risk because of inexpensive stop-loss insurance and a review of past history
4. A better design that reacts quickly to specified needs.

MODEL #2: EXECUTIVE SUMMARY

HOW RADON AFFECTS PITNEY BOWES

Radon has received much publicity in the past year. Employees in the Denver regional office took it upon themselves to test their building for radon. Readings of 35.0 pCi/l were detected. This is well above EPA threshold limits, and the employees are demanding remedial action. News of this incident will soon spread to the 509 other facilities that Pitney Bowes has throughout the United States.

The Corporate Facilities Department has requested the Corporate Safety Department to investigate a number of radon testing methods to determine the effectiveness and cost.

RADON TESTING METHODS AND COSTS

Three types of testing have been determined to meet the needs of Pitney Bowes.

1. The short-term activated charcoal method takes three to seven days and yields semi-accurate results. The cost for this method will be $7624.50.
2. The long-term alpha-track method takes three months to a year and yields accurate results. The cost for this method will be $10,174.50.
3. The on-site instantaneous method can yield very accurate results if done properly. Costs are very high, ranging from $250,000.00 to $400,000.00.

RECOMMENDATION

The Corporate Safety Department recommends that the long-term alpha-track method be used. This method combines cost efficiency and testing accuracy. A memo should be sent to all facilities to assure employees that testing will occur in the next 2 months.

MODEL #3: EXECUTIVE SUMMARY

A STRATEGIC ESS PLAN

We have developed a strategic foundation for Employee System Services (ESS) as a cornerstone to the functioning of a Human Resources Management System at each UTC Business Unit. Three important parameters are applicable to long-term strategic designs. They must be simple, flexible and stable. The Foundation has four objectives, each of which is dependent on the initiatives of the Business Units. They are:

1. Identifying human resources issues
2. Empowering human resources managers
3. Managing the implementation of technological advancements
4. Anticipating change in the dynamic and global business environment.

These objectives must function as a single unit and are not mutually exclusive. The project team has identified several critical assumptions required to achieve our objectives. These assumptions are:

- The business unit long-term strategy drives the human resources long-term strategy. The function of human resources is moving away from an administrative function and becoming a strategic business partner.
- Human resources' long-term strategy drives ESS's long-term strategy.
- ESS's customers are the supervisors and employees of UTC.
- ESS has a global perspective.

With this Strategic Foundation in place, ESS can implement action plans to provide continuous improvement to the business processes. Strategic ESS plans necessary for an effective Human Resources Management System at United Technologies Corporation include:

- Strategic training of system owners
- Organization of ESS to post-implementation needs
- Constant (and relevant) performance measurement of the system and ESS processes
- Functional and technical improvements to the system.

ESS's long-term strategy is simple, accommodates change, and provides for a stable base for the management of the system. The task assigned to ESS is both immense and complex, but ESS is creating a state-of-the-art Human Resources Management System that will create a competitive advantage for UTC.

EXERCISE **23** **Now it is time to expand your outline and write your report.** *Look at the following reports.* **They are models of the kinds of reports you should write. You should choose a topic that interests you, one that engages your energy and imagination. If the topic bores you, it will probably bore your readers as well.**

These reports are well-written and highly persuasive. One relies heavily on visuals; the other is more traditional. The first sets the scenario and answers the question "Why now?" The second puts the background information later because it is targeted at people who don't need it.

A typical proposal format can include the following:

- Statement of the Problem
- Proposed Solution
- Breakdown of all Recommendations
- Advantages / Benefits of Solution
- Time Schedule
- Methodology
- Equipment Necessary
- People Involved

PROPOSAL:
Why Start a Government Consulting Business Now?

Roger Arcand
December 1992

1.0 WHY START A GOVERNMENT CONSULTING FIRM NOW?

1.1 – GENERAL INTRODUCTION

Connecticut city and town governments have not always fully complied with state laws and regulations. Many of these oversights have resulted in revenue losses. I believe this situation is a potential business opportunity.

1.2 – COMMON ELEMENTS OF NONCOMPLIANCE

- Often the noncompliance could have been avoided.
- Most mistakes were caused by a lack of information.
- Many local government employees do not understand new laws and regulations due to a lack of training.
- Compliance with the necessary laws and regulations prevents revenue losses.

1.3 – SPECIFIC EXAMPLE

A specific example of a law that has financial impact follows:

Public Act 91.347

"An Act Concerning Computer Stored Public Records" (P.A. 91-347). As a result of this statute, public agencies must now provide copies of all data stored on a public computer if:

- a copy can be "reasonably" made
- data is not exempt under the Freedom of Information Act

Fiscal Impact

Public agencies may recover expenses by charging for:

- employee time used to provide data, not including time used to retrieve data;
- cost of engaging outside electronic copy service;
- cost of storage devices provided to the person making the request;
- computer charges incurred using the facilities of another agency or contractor to provide data.

NOTE: There is a mandate to consult with the State Office of Information and Technology (OIT) before acquiring computer hardware and software for this purpose.

| Joe Jones and the Grand List |

One day Joe Jones made a visit to the city tax assessor. His purpose was to obtain a list of all the Mercedes Benz automobiles that the city was taxing. It seemed Joe Jones felt he was paying too much tax on his beloved status symbol. Sympathetic Sally, who waited on Joe Jones, had computer anxiety. Sally asked Tom the Computer Nerd to help her with the data search. Sally did not know that she could charge for Tom's time, so she only charged Joe Jones the document reproduction fee. The moral of the story: the well-heeled Jones got a bargain, while the city lost revenue because Sally didn't fully understand the new law.

| Explanation |

Failure to recoup for information search requests/charges could easily amount to thousands of dollars a year (computer time, labor, etc.) in lost revenue.

1.4 – THE OPPORTUNITY

The inadequacies of the past offer an opportunity for a successful consulting business. I believe that the municipal consultant can build a good business by demonstrating that improved knowledge of the latest state laws and regulations can prevent revenue losses.

Strong pressure from the executive branch of state government has resulted in a decreasing public work force. With the prevailing fiscal attitude, this trend is likely to continue. Although the number of people who provide information has been reduced, the requests for that information have increased. The activity at the Connecticut Conference of Municipalities Information Service confirms the demand for this service.

2.0 THE PRODUCTS

2.1 – INFORMATION

The product of any government consulting firm is information. With a multi-layered government (i.e., Federal, State, and Local) there is a continuous flow of information. This mass of information can often become overwhelming. With the recent cutbacks in the government work force, there are fewer people to review and analyze the volumes of information generated. The objective of our new consulting firm will be to fill this void.

2.2 – HOW WILL WE DEVELOP INFORMATION ?

The consulting firm will:

- review previous cases;
- analyze the root causes of past compliance errors;
- develop a stepped approach for prevention;

- review each new law and regulation;
- develop training material for new laws and regulations.

2.3 – WHAT FORM WILL OUR PRODUCTS TAKE?

One effective way to convey information is a live oral presentation. This consulting firm should have the capacity to conduct training seminars and workshops that will familiarize local government employees with new state laws and regulations. Information given at seminars will be available on floppy disks or in hard copy.

2.4 – PRODUCT LIST

- Seminars and workshops
- Floppy diskettes (3.5 inch double-sided, double-density)
- Printed reports (hard copy)
- Information provided live (via telephone)

2.5 – PRICING

Prices are based on charges made by other consulting firms for similar services and are in the low to moderate range.

2.6 – PRICE LIST (1993)

PRODUCT	PRICE
Seminar/Workshop	$300.00 per person
Floppy disks (complete file)	$ 75.00
Printed report	$ 10.00 per page
Phone reports	$ 30.00 per hour

3.0 EQUIPMENT AND SUPPLIES

3.1 – WHAT EQUIPMENT WILL WE NEED?

Today the business of providing information is highly automated. In order to manage large amounts of information, a consulting firm should have the following equipment:

ITEM	COST	
	LOW	HIGH
• Microcomputer	$1,000.00	$3,500.00
• Laser printer	450.00	1,800.00
• Software	800.00	2,600.00
• FAX machine	1,300.00	2,400.00
• Typewriter	200.00	500.00
• Copier	800.00	1,500.00
• Calculator w/tape	25.00	40.00
• File cabinets	60.00	180.00
• Office furniture	500.00	1,200.00
• Answering machine	80.00	200.00
• Modem	500.00	1,200.00
• Miscellaneous	300.00	500.00
• Total	$6,015.00	$15,620.00

3.2 – SUPPLIES

The necessary office supplies and the estimated costs are:

SUPPLY LIST

ITEM	COST	
	LOW	HIGH
• Floppy discs	$ 150.00	$ 400.00
• Printer paper	80.00	120.00
• Subscriptions (databases)	400.00	1,200.00
• General office supplies	350.00	800.00
• Miscellaneous	100.00	300.00
• Total	$1,080.00	$2,820.00

3.3 – TOTAL COST OF EQUIPMENT AND SUPPLIES

In difficult economic times it is always wise to limit capital outlays. Purchasing only the supplies and equipment necessary to do the job in a professional manner will not jeopardize the profit potential of the new business. Therefore, start-up expenses should be kept toward the low side of the cost estimate. After studying the requirements, I feel that $10,000.00 is a reasonable amount for initial capitalization.

4.0 PERSONNEL, FACILITY AND ORGANIZATION

4.1 – PERSONNEL

In the beginning this business will need only one consultant. One researcher should be able to easily handle the anticipated volume of business. The Connecticut Conference of Municipalities Information Service, which provides information to city and town governments, receives about 10 calls a month.

The consultant should have the following abilities:

- Research skills
- Computer skills
- Presentation skills

If additional employees become necessary, the consultant will be faced with a new set of responsibilities (i.e. hiring and managing personnel). Many of the consulting firms I studied when drafting this proposal had only one to three partners, yet they did millions of dollars worth of business. Small size improves operational control and helps to make possible the effective coordination of research activities.

4.2 – FACILITY

Initially, the consulting firm should be run from the consultant's home. Operating from the home reduces the starting capital requirement, making it easier to post a near-term profit. One key advantage of an office in the home is the related federal income tax deduction.

If the business grows, a larger facility may be needed. The professional planners of the Entrepreneurial Group recommend leased space for the following reasons:

- There are many lease options.
- Many lease arrangements are flexible.
- Leased space is usually less costly than owned space.

Professional planners also caution, however, that signing a lease creates a large monthly expense that must be paid regardless of whether the business is successful or not. Telephone and utility costs are other monthly expenses that must be considered. In view of the costs, most professional advisers agree that it is preferable to start running a consulting business from your home rather than leasing space.

4.3 – ORGANIZATION

The business can operate in one of four basic forms:

- sole proprietorship
- partnership
- limited partnership
- corporation

Experts recommend limited partnerships and corporations as the best forms of organization. Both of these business arrangements limit the financial exposure of the owner and protect his or her personal assets.

Some of the key things to consider when selecting the type of operating structure are:

- tax impact;
- licensing requirements;
- use of a trademark;
- company name.

5.0 MARKETING

5.1 – HOW WILL WE MARKET THE SERVICE?

The success of marketing this service will largely depend upon the consultant's ability to find government revenue losses and bring them to the attention of the decision makers. Most decisions in local government are made by groups rather than individuals. Usually, it is the city council or the board of selectmen that determine what services a city or town will purchase. Thus, it is the city council and board of selectmen that should be targeted by the marketing campaign. Marketing should be accomplished using a personal approach. Personally contacting customers to distribute promotional material has proven to be a highly successful sales tool.

6.0 COMPETITION

6.1 – WHO IS THE MAIN COMPETITOR?

The Connecticut Conference of Municipalities Information Service is the primary competitor in this field. This organization has the advantage of being well-established and widely recognized. To compete with this organization, a new consulting firm must distinguish itself by the quality and price of its products and services. Some differences to highlight are:

CCM Information Service	Consulting Firm
• Limited product line	• Wide product line
• Annual membership fee	• Charge only for services provided
• No on-site training	• Seminars, workshops
• Scope of newsletter very wide	• A newsletter focused on new laws and regulations

7.0 PROFITABILITY

7.1 – WHAT IS THE TIMETABLE FOR PROFITABILITY?

One of the main objectives of any business venture is to make a profit. The timing of profitability is very important, because one in ten will succeed, while the other nine will fail. The income generated will depend on the ability to sell the service. As with all new concerns, it will take time to establish a client base and develop a business reputation. These elements are the keys to long-term success. For most new businesses, the first five years are very difficult. The success of the main competitor does not guarantee success for any newcomer, but it does indicate that there is a potentially lucrative business base worth competing for. The new consulting firm should recover fixed start-up expenses and begin to make money by the second year of operation.

8.0 CONCLUSION

8.1 – YOU CAN DO IT!

<u>CONCLUSIONS</u>

1. It is a good time to start a government consulting business for two main reasons:

   - the downsizing of state government;
   - the increasing complexity of state laws and regulations.

2. An opportunity exists because laws like Public Act 91-347 are always being enacted, and local employees must be trained in how to administer them correctly.
3. A new consulting business will supply information and training to city and town government employees.
4. Product diversity and quality must be the added ingredients that will distance the consultant from the competition.
5. Business start-up costs will be approximately $10,000.00.
6. The new consulting firm's first year capital expenses will be for a variety of necessary equipment and supplies.
7. The firm should be run from the home by one consultant. The prospective consultant must have research, computer and presentation skills.
8. Marketing success will depend on the consultant's ability to identify revenue loss potential and bring this to the attention of decision makers.
9. The Connecticut Conference of Municipalities Information Service is the major competitor in this business.
10. It will take at least one full year of operation before the business recovers all fixed costs and begins to show a profit.

PROPOSAL:
To Move Citicorp's Asian-Pacific Headquarters outside Hong Kong

John Rainaldi
December 1992

EXECUTIVE SUMMARY

Recommended Move of Citicorp's Asian Headquarters

Citicorp's Asian-Pacific portfolio consists of over (US) $30 billion of assets. The headquarters for Asian Pacific operations is currently located at the Citicorp Center in Hong Kong. On July 1, 1997, control of Hong Kong will transfer from Britain to the People's Republic of China.

Because of the uncertainty resulting from this transition, Citicorp should move its Asian-Pacific headquarters from Hong Kong. The new location should be Singapore.

Uncertainty about the Future

Since the Chinese takeover of Hong Kong could be beneficial for the businesses that remain, Citicorp should maintain a presence in Hong Kong by keeping a branch office there. This will allow Citicorp to capitalize on any opportunities that result from the Chinese takeover, without risking any part of the Asian-Pacific portfolio.

The Chinese say that nothing will change in Hong Kong after the takeover. This is hard to believe since the Chinese will control a capitalist economy that they know virtually nothing about. In addition, it is hard to trust the government of China after the June 4, 1989, Tiananmen Square massacre.

By moving operations, Citicorp will be one of over 70 businesses to leave Hong Kong since 1985. This number is growing rapidly, and it includes some of the largest Western firms in Southeast Asia.

Reasons to Choose Singapore

Singapore compares favorably with other potential sites, such as Thailand and Taiwan. Singapore's economic growth, geographic location and quality of available services make it the ideal new location for the Asian-Pacific headquarters.

Moving operations to Singapore is estimated to cost a total of (US) $6.5 million, which consists of $4 million in real estate costs and $2.5 million in relocation costs.

This move should be made as soon as possible, since the costs on moving will only increase over time. This is due to increasing demands for real estate as firms move to Singapore.

I. UNCERTAINTY ABOUT THE FUTURE

With an Asian-Pacific portfolio of over (US) $30 billion,[1] Citicorp is one of the major Western banking institutions in Hong Kong. In 1997, the People's Republic of China will take over control of Hong Kong. Even though this event could be a benefit to

---

[1] *Citicorp 1990 Annual Report*, Citicorp, Inc., (New York, 1991).

businesses in Hong Kong, and could open up new markets in China, **I recommend that Citicorp move its Asian-Pacific headquarters from Hong Kong to another location**.[2] The uncertainty resulting from the Chinese takeover poses too many potential threats to Citicorp's business in the Asian-Pacific region. The best way to remove this threat is to leave Hong Kong.

Even though Citicorp's Asian-Pacific portfolio includes holdings throughout the region, a significant percentage is actually in Hong Kong. Many of these holdings resulted from the actions of Citicorp's International Staff. Citicorp prides itself on this staff, which is prepared to go anywhere at anytime. The concept behind this staff is, as Chairman John Reed says, "Whatever works in New York will work in Tokyo or Hong Kong."[3] However, after the Chinese takeover, what works in New York or Tokyo may well fail in Hong Kong.

II. POSSIBLE NEW LOCATIONS FOR OPERATIONS

A. Advantages of Singapore

It is said that every loss is someone's gain. In this case, Hong Kong's loss is Singapore's gain. Many people now refer to Singapore as "the next Hong Kong." Singapore City has become the prime choice for companies bailing out of Hong Kong.[4]

Three factors have helped give Singapore one of the highest economic growth rates in the world:[5]

- Due to the Singaporian government's efforts, **Singapore has passed Hong Kong and lags only behind Tokyo in currency trade.**
- Singapore has become the leading port in Southeast Asia.
- Due in large part to the government's automated customs process, paperwork that takes several hours to process in Hong Kong takes only minutes in Singapore.

There is also another advantage to Singapore: **it is located 1,600 miles southwest of Hong Kong and is in a later time zone.** This makes Singapore's exchange markets the last to close in Southeast Asia. Traders have an extra hour to act and react at the close of the day.

---

[2] However, **I also recommend that Citicorp maintain a branch office in Hong Kong.** Please see **Appendix D** for more detail.
[3] Tichy, Noel, "Citicorp Faces the World: An Interview with John Reed," *Harvard Business Review*, Nov/Dec 1990, p. 134.
[4] Powell, Bill, "To Leave or Not To Leave," *Newsweek*, Sept. 24, 1990, p. 62.
[5] Dow Jones News Retrieval (New York, 1991).

B. Disadvantages of Singapore

However, all is not perfect in Singapore. There are questions about tight government controls there. In particular, the government has a reputation for restricting the free flow of information. In a bitter legal dispute, Dow Jones & Co. is suing the country because it restricts the circulation of *The Asian Wall Street Journal*. Even if the market is open for an additional hour, the fact that market information might not be available could amount to a competitive disadvantage.

The Singaporian government denies this charge. "We're not concerned that some bankers can't check on their portfolios first thing in the morning," says Yeo Seng Teck, leader of the Singapore Trade Development Board. "There are no restrictions on the flow of information here."[6] Of course, Mr. Yeo is a government official and is greatly interested in promoting business in Singapore. His response is not surprising. Fortunately, the Dow Jones lawsuit and continuous lobbying by the business community have convinced the Singaporian government to change many of its restrictive laws.

C. Advantages of Thailand

Many Western businesses are also moving to Thailand. Thailand's capital, Bangkok, has expanded rapidly over the past two decades, and this expansion is expected to continue. Bangkok is served by an ultra-modern airport and is located along the Chao-Pyhre River, which has ample port facilities.

The Thai government has been lifting many of its restrictive investment laws in an effort to induce foreign companies to move there. As in Singapore, economic planning has given Thailand one of the largest economic growth rates in the world.[7]

D. Disadvantages of Thailand

Thailand's economic growth, however, has caused the country to outgrow its own service capabilities. **Basic necessities such as health care and telecommunications services are in short supply.**

There are also two other major problems for Western businesses in Thailand:

- The government is a constitutional monarchy, where the King is the most beloved symbol of the nation. Power is supposed to be distributed between the Prime Minister, cabinet and legislature. In fact, **the military really controls the country.** There have been 13 *coups d'etat* since 1932. The latest was in February of 1991.

---

[6] "To Leave or Not To Leave," p. 62.
[7] Dow Jones News Retrieval, (New York, 1991).

- **The city has virtually no mass transit,** except for poor bus routes that are horribly overcrowded. The city has no subway of any kind, and, due to the low elevation and high water table, there is no way to build one. A monorail system has been discussed, but there are no plans for one.

The transportation problem has had two effects:

- It has given Bangkok a reputation for one of the world's worst traffic problems.
- It has given Bangkok an air pollution problem far greater than that in Los Angeles.

These problems can hurt day-to-day business in Bangkok. It can often take 20 minutes just to cross the street,[8] and the air quality is unhealthy. Bangkok has become one of the more popular tourist areas in Southeast Asia, but it is not an ideal place for Citicorp's new Asian-Pacific headquarters.

E. Advantages and Disadvantages of Taiwan

Many of Hong Kong's businesses are also moving to Taipei, capital of Taiwan. It is a commercial center in a fast-paced economy. As an island, Taiwan offers great ports for Western firms.

Taipei, however has many disadvantages. **Growth of the city and its economy have outpaced the growth of nearly all basic services.** It is difficult to make a simple phone call, let alone transfer computer data over phone lines. It is a crowded, over-built city that has an air quality problem nearly as bad as Bangkok's. One currency trader in Taipei recently commented that "It's not even a nice place to visit!"[9]

III. SUGGESTED NEW LOCATION

After analyzing these possible new locations, **I recommend that Citicorp move its operations to Singapore.** Singapore provides the most advantages and fewest disadvantages of the three sites proposed.

Singapore is rapidly becoming the leader in trade and finance that Hong Kong was. Over the next five-and-a-half years, Singapore is likely to grow into Southeast Asia's clear economic leader. There are concerns about the government's restriction of information, but the Dow Jones suit and lobbying by the business community are remedying this problem.

---

[8] *Video Visits: Thailand*, International Video Network (San Ramon, CA, 1989).
[9] "To Leave or Not To Leave," p. 62.

IV. FINANCIAL COST ANALYSIS

Moving an operations unit with a $30 billion portfolio is obviously expensive. In Singapore, a building that is the same size as Hong Kong's Citicorp Center would cost roughly (US) $4.5 million under current conditions. This estimate is based on the purchase of a 25 story building. Although Citicorp would use only 12 of these stories, I recommend leasing the rest to other businesses. With rent amounts in Singapore increasing, this would be a profitable investment.

Other estimated relocation costs amount to roughly (US) $2 million. This includes the cost of shipping office materials, relocating employees who remain with Citicorp, severance pay for those who don't, and other related relocation costs. Since Citicorp already has a branch office in Singapore, many of the entrance fees into the country are sunken costs.

Therefore, **total relocation costs for moving the Asian-Pacific headquarters to Singapore are estimated at (US) $6.5 million.** This is costly, but it is only 1/5 % of the total $30 billion portfolio that this move will protect.

These costs will only increase over time, since the cost of real estate in Singapore is rising rapidly due to the increased demand of businesses moving there. A further increase is possible over time if the exchange rate [currently (S) $1.66 to (US) $1.00] changes.

V. CONCLUSION

Finally, it is a sobering thought that Mr. Richard Yung chose to move his electronics firm from Hong Kong to Singapore. While it may seem unimportant that one small business moved, consider that Mr. Yung's uncle is the chairman of the China International Trade and Investment Corporation, which is the overseas investment division of the government of the People's Republic of China.

Mr. Yung's uncle is responsible for convincing businesses not to leave Hong Kong. Yet he could not convince his own nephew to stay. If Mr. Richard Yung chose to move his operation from Hong Kong to Singapore, I recommend that Citicorp do the same.

APPENDIX A
Singapore

Official Name: Republic of Singapore

Land Area: 238.6 square miles (618 square kilometers)

Capital: Singapore City, Population: 1,099,800 (1984)

People:
OVERALL POPULATION:	2,700,000 (1990)
DISTRIBUTION:	100% Urban
WORKFORCE:	1,300,000 (1989)

Education & Health:
LITERACY:	87.2%
LIFE EXPECTANCY:	Men: 71 Women: 77

Economy:
GDP (1988):	(US) $24.5 billion
FOREIGN TRADE:	(US) $33.8 billion: Imports (1989)
	(US) $35.0 billion: Exports (1989)
CHIEF TRADE PARTNERS:	USA, Japan, Malaysia
CURRENCY:	Singapore Dollar
EXCHANGE RATE to US $:	1.66 to 1.00 (11/29/91)
ECONOMIC GROWTH RATE:	9.2% (1989)
INFLATION:	2.4% (1988)
UNEMPLOYMENT:	3.3% (1988)

Government:
TYPE:	Republic
LEADER:	Prime Minister Goh Chok
LEGISLATURE:	Parliament
POLITICAL SUBDIVISIONS:	None

Other:
RAILROADS:	24 miles
ROADS:	1,699 miles
MAJOR PORTS:	1
MAJOR AIRFIELDS:	2

APPENDIX B
Thailand

Official Name: Kingdom of Thailand

Land Area: 198,115 square miles (513,115 square kilometers)

Capital: Bangkok, Population: 5,609,352 (1990)

People:	OVERALL POPULATION:	55,700,000 (1990)
	DISTRIBUTION:	18% Urban, 82% Rural
	WORKFORCE:	27,910,000 (1986)

Education & Health:	LITERACY:	88.8%
	LIFE EXPECTANCY:	Men: 62 Women: 68

Economy:	GDP (1988):	(US) $52.2 billion
	FOREIGN TRADE:	(US) $24 billion: Imports (1989)
		(US) $24 billion: Exports (1989)
	CHIEF TRADE PARTNERS:	Japan, USA, Singapore, Germany, Holland, Malaysia
	CURRENCY:	Baht
	EXCHANGE RATE to US $:	25.47 to 1.00 (11/29/91)
	ECONOMIC GROWTH RATE:	12.2% (1989)
	INFLATION:	5.4% (1988)
	UNEMPLOYMENT:	4.6% (1988)

Government:	TYPE:	Constitutional Monarchy
	LEADERS:	King Rama IX
		Interim Prime Minister Anand Panyarachun
	LEGISLATURE:	National Assembly
	POLITICAL SUBDIVISIONS:	73 Provinces

Other:	RAILROADS:	2,321 miles
	ROADS:	9,756 miles
	MAJOR PORTS:	5
	MAJOR AIRFIELDS:	4

APPENDIX C
Taiwan

Official Name: Republic of China

Land Area: 13,900 square miles (36,002 square kilometers)

Capital: Taipei, Population: 2,637,100 (1990)

People: OVERALL POPULATION: 20,200,000 (1990)
DISTRIBUTION: 71% Urban, 29% Rural
WORKFORCE: 8,460,000 (1989)

**Education
& Health:**   LITERACY: 90.8%
LIFE EXPECTANCY: Men: 71 Women: 76

Economy: GDP (1988):   (US) $150 billion
FOREIGN TRADE: (US) $49.7 billion: Imports (1988)
            (US) $60.6 billion: Exports (1988)
CHIEF TRADE PARTNERS: USA, Japan, Germany, Hong Kong
CURRENCY: New Taiwan Dollar
EXCHANGE RATE to US $:   25.76 to 1.00 (11/29/91)
ECONOMIC GROWTH RATE: 7.03% (1988)
INFLATION: 5.0% (1988)
UNEMPLOYMENT: 1.96% (1990)

Government: TYPE: Republic
LEADERS: President Lee Teng-hui
            Premier Lee Huan
LEGISLATURE: National Assembly
POLITICAL SUBDIVISIONS: 16 Counties, 2 Special
            Municipalities, 3 Municipalities

Other: RAILROADS: 2,986 miles
ROADS: 12,356 miles
MAJOR PORTS: 5
MAJOR AIRFIELDS: 2

APPENDIX D
Possible Consequences of the Chinese Takeover

There are still a great many unresolved issues about what is going to happen after the takeover. First, what is going to happen to the Hong Kong dollar? It currently takes (HK) $7.78 to equal (US) $1.00 (11/21/91 value). This rate has traditionally been stabilized by government controls. After the takeover, there is no guarantee that these controls will remain in force; the HK dollar may decline in value drastically. If this happens, it will have a devastating effect on Hong Kong's economy.

Furthermore, there is no guarantee that the HK dollar will continue to exist at all. The Chinese could decide to abandon it and convert to their own currency, a move that would also wreak havoc with the Hong Kong economy.

In addition, will the Chinese government preserve Hong Kong's liberal banking and taxation laws? These laws have traditionally been the biggest incentive for Western firms to locate in Hong Kong. If more restrictive laws are enacted, the remaining Western firms will have little reason to stay.

Finally, with so many businesses currently leaving Hong Kong, there is also the possibility of economic collapse even before the takeover. In any event, Hong Kong will ultimately have higher unemployment, and the Chinese government will have to deal with this problem while adjusting to a completely new economic system. If the situation becomes bad enough, the Chinese government could decide to change Hong Kong from a "Special Administrative Region" to a controlled economic region. This could mean the end of Hong Kong's role as an important financial market.

However, the Chinese takeover does not necessarily have to be bad. Since a great many competitors will be leaving Hong Kong, there could be an opportunity for growth. New markets could open in China, the world's most populous country and one of the most difficult for Western firms to enter successfully.

Most of the entry problems have come from government legislation. The Chinese government may reduce this legislation if they decide to implement many of the economic ideas of Hong Kong into the mainland economy. If this happens, Western firms with a Chinese presence could find themselves in a market of over one billion people and with very little competition.

For these reasons, **I recommend that Citicorp not leave Hong Kong completely.** By maintaining a branch office in Hong Kong, Citicorp will be positioned to capitalize on any opportunities that may arise.

PRINCIPLES OF

CRITICAL AND CREATIVE THOUGHT

18

PRINCIPLE

Use Rational Thought to Persuade Your Reader

We live in an age that thinks too little to be wise.

Old Chinese Proverb

Most of us never take courses in formal logic or construct syllogisms (deductive arguments). But we've all learned through experience to question our own thinking as well as the thinking of others. Most of us think we can reason and evaluate a situation before we draw a conclusion. We know something about probability and plausibility (especially in our own fields). We know which evidence is "relevant" and "irrelevant." And we also list "pros and cons" or "advantages and disadvantages" when we're conducting an argument.

But can we spot fallacious arguments? Do we understand the differences between deduction and induction? Is there a better way to structure arguments in the business world? Is there a better logical approach to business writing?

We'll answer these questions by first reviewing the old principles of formal rhetoric. Then we'll explore a newer approach derived from Stephen Toulmin, a 20th-century British philosopher.

Up until now I've been speaking to you as a business professional concerned with time, money, clarity, brevity and precision. In the next few pages, I'll be speaking more as an academic summarizing logical theory.

Aristotelian Logic

Logos, ethos and pathos, an overview of deductive logic

Aristotle tried to find causal laws operating in a universe which, in his day, seemed to be governed by mystical, supernatural powers. *Logos* was his term for the active process that discovers forms. Anything that has form becomes real or "actual."[5]

Logos, which we can translate roughly as "reason," also imprints itself on soul, which is in the body and is comprised of logical and alogical elements. The alogical elements (appetite, vegetative stasis) are in opposition to *logos*, which aims to reach the highest pleasure (contemplation of pure thought). The alogical seeks money, sex and sensual pleasures that are "unreal."

In Aristotle's hierarchy of pleasures, the highest and best activity is contemplation. In fact, contemplation is preferable to politics, war, career or other alogical pursuits. However, he did not **condemn** emotion or desire. An emotional response can often be intelligent behavior if it is open to reasoned persuasion.

Two other significant Aristotelian concepts are *ethos* and *pathos*. *Ethos*, which means roughly "character," has an important effect on the influence a speaker has over an audience. The speaker must be believable, and that quality is dependent on *ethos*. Just as *logos* is a dynamic process, so the audience is a dynamic that helps construct the proofs by which it is persuaded. Given that the entire "soul" must be addressed, the emotions, or *pathos*, must also be taken into consideration in a persuasive dialogue.[6]

[5] W.W. Fortenbaugh, *Aristotle on Emotion* (New York, 1975), pp. 1–15.
[6] *Ibid.*, pp. 17–28.

From his approach to argument, reasoning and persuasion, Aristotle developed his most important contribution to logic: the concept of the **syllogism**.[7] A syllogism is a formal, logical argument consisting of three parts: a major premise, a minor premise and a conclusion. For instance:

All men are mortal.	Major premise
Socrates is a man.	Minor premise
Therefore, Socrates is mortal.	Conclusion

Aristotle and his followers thought that all *deductive* inference is syllogistic. By setting forth valid syllogisms, they expected to avoid all fallacies. As in the example above, if a syllogism is correctly constructed, its conclusion should always be true. However, Aristotle over-estimated the value of syllogism and deduction as forms of argument. Outside of logic and pure mathematics, syllogisms hardly ever occur.[8] **In fact, nearly all the important inferences in the "real world" are *inductive* rather than deductive.** The only exceptions are in law and theology, which derive their first principles from "unquestionable" statutes and scriptures. Therefore, it is more important for us to understand how **induction** works, rather than focus on deduction and syllogism.

Induction

Let's now focus on arguments in which the premises provide **some** support, but **not conclusive** support for their conclusions. In other words, inductive arguments do not *guarantee* truth the way valid syllogisms do. Induction talks about "some" — what is true of some may be true of more — whereas deduction and syllogism speak of "all" or "many." However, induction can extend our factual knowledge, conveying new information that is not present, even implicitly, in the original premises.

Some common types of inductive arguments are:

1. arguments based on a sample

    A spot check of 1,000 1988 Fords shows there are faulty bracket welds. Therefore, everyone who owns a 1988 Ford should take it in for inspection. (Opinion polls and surveys are based on just this sort of inductive process.)

---

[7] See Appendix 4 for a summary of syllogistic logic.

[8] Bertrand Russell, *A History of Western Philosophy* (New York, 1945), pp. 198 – 202. Because of the weakness inherent in the deductive model, Russell ultimately came to the conclusion that reading Aristotle is a waste of time.

2. arguments based on causation

Since we put fluoride in the city water, there has been a marked reduction in tooth decay. (This is probably the most common form of induction. We will say more about such statements later.)

3. arguments based on past or frequent occurrences

The President walks through the Rose Garden every day at noon. It is almost noon. Therefore, he will be coming soon.

Our cable system will offer a discount during the Christmas season.

A peat bog preserves pollen in layers for thousands of years. I can show that this layer dates back to 300 B.C. Therefore, I can tell what plants grew here at that time.

There is frequently spring flooding after heavy snows. There was spring flooding in 1988, 1989 and 1990 after heavy snows. We've had heavy snows this year; therefore, there will be flooding in the spring.

4. arguments based on similarity

We tested a sample of 60 rats, giving them 400 grams of saccharine daily. All the rats developed cancer within three months. Therefore, saccharine may cause cancer in humans, as well.

Strengths of Inductive Arguments

Arguments such as the one comparing rats and humans depend heavily on the strength of the similarities. The conclusion that saccharine may produce the same physiological effects in humans as in rats assumes that the two species are essentially similar in metabolism. Of course, rats are smaller than humans. Their brains and nervous systems are less complex, etc. There are enough dissimilarities that we must use the word "may" in comparing their reactions. In general, such comparisons between essentially dissimilar objects that share some similarities are called *metaphorical analogies*.[9]

The stronger the similarities, the stronger the analogy. By the same token, the greater the number of relevant dissimilarities, the weaker the argument is.

[9] Merrilee H. Salmon, *Logic and Critical Thinking* (New York, 1989), pp. 48–49.

Metaphor, in one sense, is a "dehydrated" analogy. If I say, "My sister is a pig," I am comparing qualities from the domain of "pigness" to qualities in the human realm (sloppiness, filthiness, greediness, smelliness).

Lois Bueler points out that there is a sharp distinction between metaphoric analogy and what I will call "lateral" analogy, an extension of abstract description. *Whereas metaphor expresses a relationship about qualities, "lateral" analogy expresses a relationship about relationships*:

No productive nation can afford too many drones.

This comparison is more complex: the relationship between drones and worker bees is mapped onto the relationship between unproductive and productive people. This form of analogy is a very different matter from mere resemblance.[10]

1. **Simile**: Your lips are like roses.
2. **Metaphoric analogy**: My sister is a pig.
3. **Lateral analogy**: No productive nation can afford too many drones.

The strength of analogy in an argument is similar to the strength of its metaphors and similes. If the metaphor is dead (the leg of a chair), we don't notice it. If it is alive (my sister's piglet face), we can see and hear and feel the comparison and accept its truth.

What also strengthens strong metaphoric analogy is the number and the relevance of the similarities between the objects compared. If my sister has a "snout" for a nose and she is fat with pinkish skin, the physical similarities add to the psychological portrait we've formed in our minds.

---

[10] Lois Bueler, *What We Do When We Think: Analogies and Test Cases*, a paper given at the CCCC Conference in Chicago, March 1990.

EXERCISE **24** **Let's look at the following analogies to decide what kind they are and whether or not they are effective. What kind of analogies are used here? Could they be improved? How?**

1. Economists use metaphors to establish basic theories about how economies work. The economy is like the seasons and will have similar recurring cycles. In 1990, just as in 1929, a severe recession followed on the heels of market prosperity.

    Were the same factors operating that were operating in 1929? Take a pro or con position and argue the analogy between 1990 and 1929.

2. In the movie, "Being There," Peter Sellers compares the political world with a garden world where he lived as a recluse. A simple gardener, he is hit by a car and taken to the home of a wealthy political figure. He makes a great impression speaking the language he knows, the language of planting and harvesting and the changing seasons.

    Following this example, create a metaphoric analogy or a lateral analogy.

3. Is the national or state debt like private debt? If so, construct an analogic argument.

4. Develop an oral presentation that relies heavily on graphic language (word pictures). Choose an evocative metaphor. Get your audience to see what you want them to see, feel what you want them to feel. Your topic can be any of the following:

    a. the present or future challenges of cultural diversity in your company.
    b. the problem of AIDS or drug abuse in your company.
    c. the rising cost of health care benefits and the necessity of employees sharing the burden.
    d. downsizing plans that will affect your department.
    e. the lack of day care facilities in your company.

In summary, in the real world we mostly argue from particulars, concrete instances. The evidence builds up until we form a generalization: a movement from specifics to a general conclusion. But what can go wrong with this inductive process? As we've stated, the premises provide <u>some</u> support but not <u>irrefutable</u> support for the conclusions. There is less certainty than in deductive reasoning. However, in deductive reasoning, you can have a totally false premise: Women can't lead a major corporation. She's a woman; therefore, she can't be a good CEO.

What can go wrong in an inductive argument?

The structure of an inductive argument (what is true of some may be true of more or all) depends upon three factors:

1. The size of the sample
   How many rats do we test? How many times has the President walked through the Rose Garden at noon? How many times have we tested pollen samples in peat bogs? How many autos have we checked for faulty bracket welds?

2. The quality of the sample
   Are rats the best animals to compare with humans? Shouldn't the scientists use monkeys instead? Is this peat bog truly frozen in time or were layers removed? Did the autos we tested come from one city or from many cities? Were they produced by one factory in Wisconsin or several factories?

3. The truth of the evidence
   Is the dosage of saccharine so high that it would be impossible for any human to ingest so much saccharine on a given day?

   Could several different types of trees give off the same pollen? Did we leap to a hasty conclusion because a few cars had loose bracket welds? Could these loose welds be caused by the stress of severe winter conditions in the town of Boulder where the cars were examined?

We are constantly thinking analogically in a sloppy sense, i.e., we are:

comparing: (creating parallels). We gave money to Zimbabwe for oral rehydration, and it worked. Therefore we should give money to Angola for the same purpose.

classifying: This depressed person is like that depressed person. Therefore, he belongs in the same hospital ward.

judging: You broke down under stress last year. Therefore you should not be running for higher office this year.

Yet many of these conclusions are faulty because no two situations are exactly alike, and no two humans are exactly alike, and no individual is exactly the way he was a year ago. Time has passed, bringing the possibility for change.

We will discuss in more detail some of the fallacies associated with inductive generalities. Remembering these few caveats about the weaknesses of analogic induction, let's look at the more complex question of **causal claims**.

Causal claims: A special case

Some causal claims take the form of inductive generalizations; others are arguments from analogy. In ordinary life, we look for causal connections when cars break down, when classes are cancelled, when we do poorly in an examination, or when personal relationships change. **Spontaneous causal analysis is remarkably common in ordinary conversation.**[11]

In one experiment, investigators "bugged" conversations at singles' bars, at a picnic for economically underprivileged senior citizens, and at student "bull" sessions. They found that each utterance could be classified into a set of categories that included:

1. informing
2. evaluating
3. advising
4. predicting
5. analyzing.

While causal analysis constituted 15% of all utterances recorded, this does not mean that cause is always present. Correlation is **not** causation.[12]

---

[11] R. Nisbett and L. Ross, *Human Inference* (Englewood Cliffs, 1980), p. 80.

[12] Marvin Minsky, *The Society of Mind* (New York, 1985), p. 48, notes that we usually think in terms of causes, similarities, and dependencies. Whenever we can, we like to explain things in terms of cause and effect. However, in real life the causal relationships are rarely singular or simple.

Of course, the scientist can prove cause because he can control the number of variables in an experiment. But in the human laboratory, what looks like cause and effect (A causes B) is often just an argument from **sign**: One situation is the **sign** of another.

> If a thermometer reads twenty below zero, it is a **sign** that the lake is frozen, not the cause of the freezing.

Most causal situations are complex, as everyone knows from watching murder trials on television or understanding the difference between **proximate cause** and the causal chain:

> Max is accused of shooting Tony, and Tony dies. The medical doctor will say that Tony died of "massive internal bleeding." If Tony dies on the operating table, the cause may be suffocation. But the true cause that led to the suffocation (which is the proximate cause, the cause nearest the event) is Max's gun. The law is only interested in one part of the causal chain: who gets punished.

In the business world, we must be careful when we use the word "cause." It is far closer to the truth to use the word "indicate":

> The thermometer reading of 20 below zero **indicates** that the lake is frozen.
> The fact that I can't button my pants **indicates** that I have gained weight.
> The high volume of rising issues on the stock exchange **indicates** a healthy economy.

Does A cause B? Or does B cause A? The student (A) wanted to go home because he was tired of working (B). The student was tired of work (B) because he wanted to go home (A).

The student could start out with both a distaste for work and an inclination to go home. Then a loop of circular causality ensues, and the combined urge becomes irresistible. Minsky talks a lot about causal loops, mazes, and simple chains. When we "straighten out" our thinking, we isolate these chains of causes and effects. That often oversimplifies the situation since the looping of many chains is the real causality.

For example: A heat wave in the middle of February that is recordbreaking might be caused by the "greenhouse" effect. On the other hand, it might be caused by a localized air current. Or it might be caused by both. Of course, it might also be a one-time occurrence. Or it could be connected with pollution from blazing forests in the Amazon. Nuclear waste burning on a Pacific island? All of these? Some of these? None of these?

EXERCISE **25** Examine the following arguments to determine if causation is at work. Is there a causal link, or is it simply that one situation is the sign of another?

1. In 1940 there was a measles epidemic in the spring. In 1941 there was a measles epidemic in the spring. In 1942 there was a measles epidemic in the spring. In 1943 there was a measles epidemic in the spring. Therefore, in 1944 there will be a measles epidemic in the spring.

2. The new family next door must be nice; they have a lighted Christmas wreath in every window.

3. New management decides to raise the lights in a factory. Productivity increases. Management then lowers the lights in the same factory. Productivity increases. Raising the lights seems to cause increases, but so does lowering the lights.

The Stephen Toulmin Model: Claim, Evidence and Rationale

As I've said, many people never study logic. They don't know the difference between induction and deduction, and they construct arguments according to prescribed formats, filling in the blanks with relevant data. However, when they have to come up with something new, to think through a fresh problem, they are often lost as to how to begin.

But there is a simpler method of organizing thought — a condensed version of the work of Stephen Toulmin. Toulmin, a contemporary British logician, showed that the criteria used to judge arguments is "field dependent," that the grounds for arguments differ from field to field. Toulmin uses two terms: <u>claim</u> and <u>data</u> (evidence). Raw data means nothing until we know why it should be accepted as evidence for a claim.

Toulmin calls his defense the <u>warrant</u>, a guarantee that the data is relevant to the claim. We could call it the <u>authority</u> that differs from field to field. In law, the <u>authority</u> is a principle embodied in the statutes that connects the evidence to the claim. What I hope to show is that the <u>authority</u> can be seen also as an inductive or deductive rationale (logical principle) that brings evidence to bear on the claim. Therefore, let's begin with three terms (Claim, Evidence, Rationale) used in a very special sense:

Claim

This is the point you want to prove. It is what you want the reader to accept as:

1. true or not true
2. of a certain kind or not of that kind
3. good or bad
4. worth doing or not worth doing

Claims answer the questions:

1. Is it true?
2. What kind is it?
3. What is its quality?
4. What should be done about it?

All arguments are developed as answers to these questions.

Examples of claim #1 (is it true?) could be:

a. Mr. Smith exceeded the speed limit.
b. The local bookstore made a profit.
c. The cost of living is increasing.

Examples of claim #2 (what kind is it?) could be:

a. Mr. Smith committed first degree murder when he took his ailing wife's life.
b. The bookstore is in trouble because of the recession or because it fails to stock the books the neighborhood wants to read.
c. A 10% decline in the dollar is needed to constitute true inflation.

Examples of claim #3 (what is its quality?) could be:

a. Mr. Smith's action was good in that he was putting a terminally ill loved one out of her misery.
b. The bookstore should carry pornography if there are people in the neighborhood who want it.
c. We need a state income tax that is graduated, not a flat rate that would be equal for everyone.

Examples of claim #4 (is it worth doing?) could be:

a. Mr. Smith is guilty of first degree murder. He should be executed.
b. The local bookstore should be closed because it carries pornography.

c. Because the cost of living is increasing, I should get a raise this year from my company.

Evidence

You must present evidence to support your claim just as you need pilings planted in a river bed to support a bridge. What links the <u>evidence</u> to the <u>claim</u> is the steel superstructure rising above the pilings. That superstructure is the **rationale**. It is the logical principle that creates the link between evidence and claim:

Figure 18-1

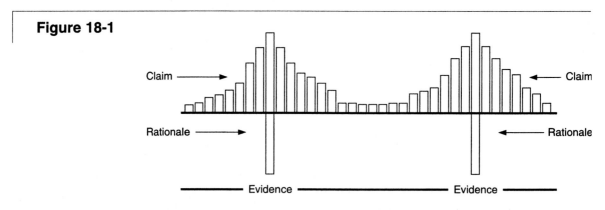

Evidence can be observed facts, statistics, exhibits, opinions, or predictions accepted as true by your audience. There are many tests to determine whether the quality of evidence:

1. Tests for observed facts:

   Is the observer credible? biased? qualified?
   Was there **direct** observation?
   Did the observer's attitude color his perception?
   Under what circumstances was the observation made?

2. Tests of statistical evidence:

   Do the statistics come from a credible source?
   Do they cover a significant size? sufficient time?
   Does the reporting method mask variations in the data?

3. Tests of exhibits:

   Is the exhibit genuine?
   Is the exhibit typical of the phenomena it represents?

4. Tests of opinion:

Is the statement biased?
What is the background of the opinion maker?
Does the opinion maker have a successful track record?

5. General tests:

Is the evidence consistent with other evidence?
Is the statement consistent with itself?
Is it consistent with human nature or other predictable norms?
Is the evidence clearly and objectively presented?

NOTE: Evidence must be acceptable to your audience. Fact and truth are relative matters. Even if you are convinced of the truth of your claim and the soundness of your evidence, if your audience doesn't accept your evidence as true, you cannot persuade them.

If you feel that your evidence will not be acceptable because of your audience's belief system, you must treat the evidence as a claim and prove its unshakable truth.

Rationale

Rationale is the authority or logical principle that connects the evidence to the claim.

There are approximately seven rationales commonly used in analysis and argument. The nature of your evidence will reveal which of the seven rationales you will employ to allow your claim to rest on a solid foundation. You should also be aware that each rationale has its characteristic weakness. These weaknesses are listed after each rationale.

1. What is true of some may be true of more or all.

"A survey of some 1,500 complaints indicates that 40% stemmed from dissatisfaction with N division. No other division was the object of more than 5% of the complaints. Consequently, to improve our customer relations fastest, we should concentrate on N division."

Weakness: The first rationale is no stronger than its sample. A flawed sample will result in a faulty argument.

2. What is true of many or all is true of some.

"**Many** 1977 Model 72-A's have been faulty. So you should take yours in for inspection."

"**All** 1977 Model 72-A's have been recalled because of faulty bracket welds. So you should take yours in for repair."

Weakness: The second rationale runs into difficulty because one has to determine what is true of many or all. One can rarely survey every instance, and so one can rarely know the facts about every member of a class. And even if you know that something is true of many members of a class, the sample you are studying may not be representative of the "many."

3. Two cases are parallel.

"We seem unable to get important decisions made quickly and made right. Xerox had the same problem and solved it through decentralization. We should decentralize our management too."

Weakness: The third rationale stumbles because two cases are never wholly parallel.

4. All the alternative claims that would account for the evidence are false.

"Since the weather has been bitterly cold, there will be a shortage of fuel oil because oil companies don't have extra stock in storage and because ice is hampering transportation by rail, truck and barge."

Weakness: The fourth rationale falters whenever someone states a claim you had not foreseen.

5. One situation is the cause of another.

"When we installed the 42 system, our output doubled. Since that was the only change, the system was responsible for the increase."

Weakness: The fifth rationale must contend with a basic weakness. When we see X as the cause of Y, we never really see X causing Y. What we actually see is that X always comes first and that Y always follows X. So we assume that they are linked, and we say "X causes Y." But this linkage could always be a coincidence or an illusion.

6. One situation is the sign of another.

"Bradley was manager when the system was installed. The doubling of his staff's output shows he's a good manager."

Weakness: The sixth rationale is a safer argument than the fifth, but it is weaker.

7. Two cases are analogous.

"A good manager is a blocking back whenever and wherever needed. No job is too menial for him if it helps one of his players advance toward his objective."

Weakness: The seventh rationale becomes weak when the two objects or examples being compared are too dissimilar.

Some people find it difficult to distinguish between evidence and the rationale (the logical principle that connects the evidence to the claim). Here are a few examples of claim, evidence and rationale:

Figure 18-2

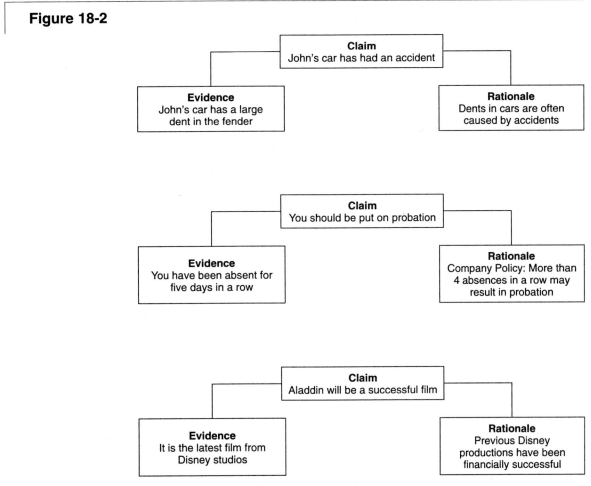

Claim
John's car has had an accident

Evidence
John's car has a large dent in the fender

Rationale
Dents in cars are often caused by accidents

Claim
You should be put on probation

Evidence
You have been absent for five days in a row

Rationale
Company Policy: More than 4 absences in a row may result in probation

Claim
Aladdin will be a successful film

Evidence
It is the latest film from Disney studios

Rationale
Previous Disney productions have been financially successful

Sometimes your evidence will contain claims. If so, you may have to support that evidence with further evidence and rationales.

Figure 18-3

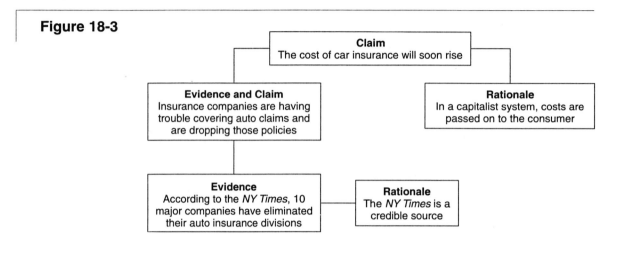

Summary of Toulmin Logic

Claim

Your claim is the point you want to prove. You want to convince your readers, or listeners, that your claim is true.

Claims assert that something was, is, or will be:

- true or not true
- of a certain kind or not of that kind
- good or bad
- worth doing or not worth doing.

Evidence

Your evidence is information or judgments that you think your audience will accept as true.

Evidence can be:

- reports
- statistics
- exhibits
- predictions.

Rationale

Since your audience won't automatically believe your claim, how can your evidence compel them to see your claim as true? Obviously your evidence must relate to your claim in such a way that accepting the evidence will compel people to accept the claim too. That principle of relationships is the rationale. The rationale is the principle that you use to try to make your audience accept your claim if they accept your evidence.

So we have **claim**, **evidence** and **rationale**. In theory, it's as simple as that. In practice, it's sometimes a bit more puzzling.

First, what happens if, for instance, I disagree with you? I will challenge your rationale, your evidence, or both. I will challenge them because I know that if I accept them, I will have to accept your claim. So when I challenge them, you have to turn them into claims and support them in turn with additional evidence and rationales. Once you have won these subordinate arguments, you can go on with the argument you were originally making.

Second, suppose you think that I am already convinced that one part of your argument is true. You might then choose to leave it out. People often leave parts of arguments unstated.

For example: *Since the cost of steel is rising, the price of new cars will rise.*

The first part of the sentence is a piece of evidence; the second is the claim. What is the rationale? Doesn't the argument assume that all the alternative claims that would account for the evidence are false? For instance, the argument implies that the following claims (in italics) are false:

Although the cost of steel is rising, *manufacturers can cut costs elsewhere.*

Although the cost of steel is rising, *manufacturers will absorb the increases themselves.*

If you know little about prices, and the costs of cars, and the history of the auto industry, you might accept these alternatives. But if you are knowledgeable about the industry (that manufacturers never seem to cut costs and absorb increases) the alternatives will seem improbable, and you will accept the claim that car prices are going to rise.

Now let's look at some examples of real world writing to see if they illustrate the principles of **claim**, **evidence** and **rationale**. The first is a "before and after" of a legal rebuttal.

Before

In rebuttal of the claimant's contention regarding the alleged denial of the time off for the religious holidays, the employer at one point stated, "We wouldn't be that stupid," or words to that effect. Moreover, it is established that arrangements for a substitute had already been made. It appears clear beyond cavil that a reasonable individual would be aware of the impropriety of refusing time off requested in accordance with an employee's religious beliefs. Additionally, there is substantial evidence of a more obvious motivation for the claimant's voluntary separation: her dissatisfaction with the terms of the contract. This Referee, therefore, concludes that the claimant was not in fact denied the requested time off and that her voluntary separation was the result of her dissatisfaction with the terms of her employment.

After

Claim: The claimant terminated her employment due to dissatisfaction with her job. She did <u>not</u> leave because she was denied time off for religious holidays.

Evidence:

1. The employer stated "We wouldn't be that stupid."
2. The employer had already made arrangements for a substitute.
3. A reasonable individual would understand that employers don't refuse time off for observation of religious holidays.
4. There is substantial evidence of a more obvious motive: the claimant's dissatisfaction with the terms of the contract.

Rationale: Therefore, the evidence does not support claimant's explanation for her termination. (All of the alternative claims that would account for the evidence are false.)

EXERCISE **26**

I. This example is an argument that involves a simple claim: You are placed on probation. Look at the following sentences and decide if they are evidence or rationales. Place E or R beside each number. Remember, the evidence is usually a recitation of verifiable facts, and the rationale gives an underlying reason or principle behind the action.

_____ 1. You were absent five days in March.

_____ 2. We discussed your previous absences in February, and I warned you that if you continued your absences, you would be placed on probation.

_____ 3. The company policy states that if you're absent for five days in one month without necessary causes, you must be placed on probation.

II. Treat the following three sentences as a single argument. Decide if they are claim, evidence or rationale and place C, E or R before each number.

_____ 1. I don't feel it's necessary to microfilm letters that are over 6 months old.

_____ 2. It is time-consuming and too expensive to be used only a few times.

_____ 3. We microfilmed six months of correspondence, and those tapes were used only five times.

III. Look at the following sentences and decide if they are claims, evidence or rationales. Sentences 1 – 7 comprise a single paragraph; you should treat them as one argument. Place C, E or R beside each number.

_____ 1. Your recent absences and an alert we received from personnel have caused us to review your attendance.

_____ 2. During the period from March 1978 through September, you have been absent for nine days in five periods.

_____ 3. Combining the days and periods of absence gives a total of 14.

_____ 4. In your new job, you have been absent six days in three periods for a total of nine.

_____ 5. According to Corporate policy, a combination of days and periods that exceeds 15 during the course of a whole year is less than satisfactory attendance.

_____ 6. You are in danger of exceeding these limits in the period of a half year.

_____ 7. This memo is formal notice that further absences may be considered grounds for instituting formal probationary action.

IV. Identify the kind of rationale in each sample. NOTE: Not all of the kinds are used, and some may be used more than once. Remember the 7 types of rationale: 1. induction, 2. deduction, 3. parallel, 4. alternative claims, 5. causal, 6. sign, 7. analogy

_____ 1. There are many reasons that can explain the failure to produce large-scale housing programs. The failure to marshall the required resources is clearly one of the most important.

_____ 2. Again, the studies conducted by our firm indicate that the problem is not one of increasing subsidies as much as it is one of targeting them correctly.

_____ 3. These conditions appear to constitute for many governments a housing problem beyond a solution. The case of Sri Lanka, however, offers an interesting example of how one government is attempting with limited resources to address the central question of providing affordable shelter for its population at scale.

_____ 4. I recommend changing the term "fair share" to two levels of giving: Sponsor and Patron. We conducted a survey to see if this change would confuse people. Of the 119 responses, only three were confused about the change. Therefore I conclude that the change will not confuse our employees.

_____ 5. During the 1980s, rate regulation was a turbulent sea, companies struggled to keep afloat, buffeted by the tidal wave of competitive pricing.

EXERCISE **26**
(concluded)

6. Many towns are having difficulty with waste problems. Windham is now considering many options for dealing with its problem. These options include:

- Turn control of the facility over to the state.
- Tear the facility down and build a new plant.
- Modernize the existing facility.

We recommend modernizing the facility since Avon did this successfully.

7. The conference was held behind closed doors. The attorney kept only handwritten notes. The only participants were officers of the company who had been directly involved in the transaction. All these factors indicate that the parties intended the meeting to be confidential.

8. Defense argues that riding in the back of a pickup truck is like failure to wear a seatbelt, which cannot be contributory negligence under Connecticut statute. But riding in the back of a truck is factually different from not wearing a seatbelt. Such riding increases the likelihood of a foreseeable injury. Wearing a seatbelt does not. Therefore, the evidence does not support the counterclaim.

As we've just seen, the identification of claim, evidence and rationale can structure your argument before you begin to write. The errors to avoid are:

1. Putting the claim last.
2. Leaving out the rationale.
3. Mixing the three elements so that the reader's mind does not grasp the various points of the argument.

Now that we're familiar with this structure of argument, let's look at how it can be applied to produce excellent writing. Using the Claim, Evidence and Rationale structure, study the following "before and after" memo to see how the original has been improved.

Before

Although reasons for continued AID population support to the LAC middle-income countries for Brazil, Colombia and Mexico are varied due to special circumstances in each, the basic policy guidance flows from Attachment A "A strategy for a More Effective Bilateral Development Assistance Program: An A.I.D. Policy Paper" sent to the field in AIDTO A-168, April 6, 1978, as part of the FY 1980 Program Guidance.

Section III C p. 40 on program implications of assistance to middle-income countries, indicates that a basic needs oriented approach does not rule out middle-income countries for assistance because, in general, they still have a great many poor people. The poor of Brazil, Mexico and Colombia outnumber the poor found in a great many smaller countries in Africa, for example. Programs to carry out this policy would focus in those areas such as population, where AID has expertise, and emphasize strengthening the scientific and technological capabilities of middle-income countries. Population assistance would be aimed at the poor by expanding the provision of safe, effective, affordable and acceptable family planning services. This would be carried out by developing community based systems for distribution of family planning supplies, training of personnel in modern techniques of contraception, development of information and programs, and provision of low-cost contraceptives. Support activities in data collection and analysis, policy development, biomedical and operations research would be improved as well.

Attachment B, "Briefing Paper on Population for the Administrator's Retreat, June 20, 1981" reiterates many of the conclusions found in the "Global 2000 Study" that shows the environmental degradation and impact on economic growth of continued rates of population growth.

One of the points that emerges from this piece is that awareness of the population problem has risen in the LDC's during the seventies to the point that appropriate use of modern contraceptive technologies now is creating a substantial demand for programs which transfer these technologies. The U.S. is receiving requests for support from countries such as Brazil and Mexico, which until fairly recently felt they had no population problem. The progressive deterioration in their ability to deal with thousands of unemployed young people, huge numbers of children and families, within their development budgets, has led them to the realization that family planning services now are required to stem the tide by the year 2000.

Mr. ———, Assistant Administrator for Latin America, testified before the Subcommittee on Inter-America Affairs House International Relations Committee on March 2, 1978 (Attachment C) and laid out well the case for a middle-income country strategy on p. 11–14. His statement included — "Many countries are encountering increasingly difficult 'second generation' problems as they move along the stages of development. Foremost among these problems is that of how to manage an economy so as to keep it growing and stable, while engaging in social reform. Equally unavoidable technological problems that arise as development progresses include the conservation-development trade-off urban growth and blight, national technology equal to the design and production of goods competitive in world trade, environmental problems, and inadequacies in science and technology education and research. Note that this statement predated the revolution in Nicaragua, the conflict in El Salvador and current problems in Guatemala; all countries overwhelmed with population growth rates over 3% annually and sluggish economies.

Based on this background, the rationale for population assistance activities in three of Latin America's largest countries becomes much clearer. What are the special circumstances that create AID's need to fund sizeable population assistance programs in Brazil, Colombia and Mexico.

MEXICO
President Jose Lopez Portillo moved rapidly to install a vigorous and effective family planning program after taking power in December 1976. All public health organizations were united under a new Coordinating Commission for family planning programs and a policy established to reduce the annual

population growth rate from 3.5% to 2.6% by the end of the presidential term. Our Embassy was informed that Mexican institutions were prepared to accept assistance in this program from international agencies to provide training, equipment, supplies, information and education support, research, and data collection activities in a massive effort to get this program underway. U.S. input was determined to be appropriate in supporting a close neighbor to deal with a problem that also had an impact on our country. The GOM support to the program annually has been twenty to thirty times that which we have provided.

At this point, it is clear that Mexico will reach its growth rate target for 1982 of 2.6%, now the goal is 2% by 1990 and 1% in 2000. Over 40% of families are using modern methods of contraception and all public health agencies have trained staffs and equipment in place to carry out the program. New requirements have been forged to carry the service delivery through the public structure to isolated sections of the country and institutionalize the technology transfer in the country's training and research agencies. An effort to develop a nation-wide private sector service structure is being carried out to insure that private family planning services are available in case of changes in government policy. Logistics support continues to supply program needs that are not yet covered by GOM support. The program works well, but is not yet reaching all of Mexico's poor population.

BRAZIL
This country is the sixth largest in the world with 30% of Latin America's population. The impact of Brazil's 2.8% annual population growth rate is seen in an infant mortality rate of 109 per 1000 live births, an estimated 2,000,000 abandoned children, a requirement to create about 1,500,000 new jobs annually and rapid growth rates in large urban centers. Brazil's President Joao Baptista de Oliveira Fiqueiredo on assuming office in March 1979 stated, "In the present situation of Brazil, the success of social development programs depends in large part on family planning, but always respecting the couple's freedom of choice."

This changed attitude led the U.S. Embassy to submit a strategy supporting development of family planning service activities primarily in the private sector and focusing on the Northeastern area of the country and selected urban areas. The program focused on training, equipment, development of low cost delivery systems and some supporting services in data collection, research, and institutional development. The program got underway later than the Mexico effort. But already impact is evident in the rapidly growing discussion in Brazil's Congress for more government effort and simplification of laws surrounding contraception. Brazil will probably host a Latin American meeting of parliamentarians of Population and Development next year. Probably two million families have now been provided with modern contraception and are currently planning their families. Because of its size, this effort to transfer technologies to Brazil has a long way to go before it is in place nationwide. U.S. inputs here are not as large as in Mexico and thus have had a more limited impact; however a great many additional needs are identified and could be programmed rapidly should funds become available.

COLOMBIA
This country has received U.S. population assistance, mostly through intermediaries, since 1967 and has reduced its crude birth rate from 44.0 per 1000 in 1966 to an estimated 27.0 per 1000 in 1980. Both the Government of Colombia and the private sector have followed a rigorous policy of trying to provide family planning services to all couples who request it. The goal is to reduce the current 1.9% annual growth rate to 1.0% as soon as possible. Assistance to this stable democracy and its success in its efforts at population growth reduction have increasingly been used as an example and regional training ground for family planners from all over the region. Its programs of innovative delivery systems, voluntary sterilization, training of auxiliary workers, commercial retail sales, and family planning management have provided real examples of how to accomplish population programs.

However, Colombia's program is heavily dependent on the IPPF affiliate PROFAMILIA. Although this institution raises 25% of its funds locally, it receives no GOM subsidy and local tax laws do not support charity giving. With approximately two thirds of the family planning acceptors, the reduction in U.S. intermediary support to the Agency proposed by the U.S. Embassy with elimination by 1985 poses serious problems to population technicians concerned with program continuity. It is unclear at this point what the outcome will be, but reductions to date have led the FPA to higher fee for services charges and resulting decline in services particularly to the rural poor. The GOC Ministry of Health is managing to move its program into national budget support, but also has problems in maintaining the contraceptive supply levels it requires. With per capita income of slightly over $900, Colombia may provide a case study in how difficult it will be to phase out population assistance to middle income countries.

After

TO: William Hanson
FROM: Carl Larrette
SUBJECT: LATIN AMERICAN MIDDLE INCOME POPULATION STRATEGY

INTRODUCTION:

AID's policy of support for population programs in middle-income Latin American countries flows from the FY 1980 Program Guidance, sent to the field in 1978 (see Attachment A).

STRATEGY RECOMMENDATION: **AID should continue supporting population programs in middle-income Latin American countries.**

REASONS:

A. **There are more poor people in Brazil, Mexico and Colombia than in many smaller African states**. Thus a basic needs approach is compatible with population assistance to these countries. Assistance would be focused on strengthening host country technical expertise and on expanding the provision of family planning services to the poor.

B. **Continued population growth slows economic growth and contributes to environmental degradation**. Attachment B, "Briefing Paper on Population for the Administrator's Retreat" explains this relationship. His conclusions are the same as those in the "Global 2000 Study."

C. **Middle-income countries in Latin America are now requesting more population assistance than before**. Use of modern contraceptive technologies is creating a demand for programs that transfer them. We are receiving requests for support from Brazil and Mexico which, until recently, felt they had no problem. They are now experiencing a progressive deterioration in their social, political, and financial ability to deal with thousands of unemployed young people and huge numbers of children.

D. **Middle-income countries are experiencing "second generation" problems in their development processes**. Mr. X, Assistant Administrator for Latin America, outlined these problems in his testimony before Congress in 1978 (see Attachment C). He described, among others, the difficulty of balancing economic growth and social reform, the conservation-development trade-off, urban growth and blight, and scientific inadequacies.

ACHIEVING STRATEGY GOALS:

AID's strategy of providing population assistance to middle-income countries in Latin America is designed to work by:

A. **Developing community-based systems for distribution of family planning supplies.**
B. **Training personnel in modern techniques of contraception.**
C. **Developing information and education programs.**
D. **Providing low-cost contraceptives.**
E. **Supporting data collection and analysis, policy development, and operations research activities.**

BACKGROUND:

MEXICO

Relevant History: President Lopez Portillo rapidly installed a vigorous and effective family planning program after his election in 1976. His goal was to reduce annual population growth from 3.5% to 2.6% by the end of his term. We have provided a wide variety of assistance to the government. Mexico will reach its growth rate target by the end of this year.

Current Effort: Mexico's new population growth rate goal is 2% by 1990 and 1% by 2000. More than 40% of families are using modern contraceptive methods. All public health agencies have trained staffs and equipment in place. The government is extending services to the more isolated areas of the country. Private sector programs are beginning in case of shifts in government policy. The major problem is to extend family planning services to all of Mexico's many poor.

BRAZIL

Relevant History: Brazil has 30% of the population of Latin America and a high (2.8%) rate of population growth. President Fiqueiredo supports family planning as long as it respects the couple's freedom of choice. This is a significant change of attitude in Brazil.

Current Effort: The U.S. supports the extension of family planning services through the private sector. Urban areas and the Northeast are the principal targets. The program focuses on training, equipment, development of low cost delivery systems, and institutional development. About two million Brazilian families now plan their families with modern contraceptives. Brazil has a long way to go, however. U.S. inputs are smaller than those in Mexico. Additional needs have been identified and could be programmed rapidly if funds become available.

COLOMBIA

Relevant History: The U.S. has aided Colombia's population program since 1967. The crude birth rate has fallen during this period, from 44 per 1000 to 27 per 1000. The government and the private sector are committed to reducing the current 1.9% annual growth rate to 1.0% as soon as possible.

Current Effort: Colombia is an example of a highly successful population control effort. Its programs of innovative delivery systems, voluntary sterilization, training of auxiliary workers, commercial retail sales, and family planning management serve as a training ground for regional family planners. The major problem facing the Colombian program is its significant dependence of PROFAMILIA, the IPPF affiliate. This organization is substantially U.S. funded. The U.S. Embassy is planning to reduce this support and to eliminate it by 1985. The impact of this on Colombia's program will be severe.

NOTE: Even in a prescribed format, you can improve your writing:

Before

Rate Actions: Timeliness

The current timeliness ratio is based on a model containing an average of 6 rate actions per month. With an allowance for an unscheduled or additional 7th rate action not being on time, the present timeliness ratio of 6/7, or 86% was established. From January 1987 to October 1988 the average number of rate actions has decreased to approximately 3.5 per month. The average number of rate actions during the period November 1987 to October 1988 was 2.5 per month for CARS and 3.5 per month for HARIS, for a 3.0 per month average over both systems. This trend is expected to continue in the near future. As Data Processing is staffed in accordance with the volume of work, and rate actions are tracked against statutory or filed effective date and not scheduled implementation date, (lateness can be the result of ISO, legislative or "user" delays as well as programming delays), it continues to be important for the standard to allow for an additional work request not being completed by the statutory or filed effective date. Therefore, the revised model would contain an average of 3 rate actions per month, an allowance for an additional 4th rate action not on time, resulting in a recommendation for a timeliness ratio of 3/4 or 75%.

After

Rate Actions: Timeliness

The present timeliness ratio should change from 6/7 or 86% to 3/4 or 75%.

REASONS

1. The present model is based on 6 actions/month with an unscheduled 7th (6/7 or 86%).

2. The trend has been approximately 3.5 per month from January 1987 to October 1988.

   From November 1987 to October 1988 the average was 2.5 for CARS and 3.5 for HARIS for a 3.0 monthly average for both systems. We think this trend will continue.

3. We still have to allow for additional work requests, hence the recommendation of 3 rate actions with an additional 4th (3/4 or 75%).

We've looked at many "befores and afters" of real-world writing. Now let's look at an example of excellent writing by a young business student:

PROPOSAL For parents to loan $2300 to their son for purchase of a personal computer. This loan will have deferred payments and low interest rate.

WHY A PERSONAL COMPUTER IS NEEDED

1. **Many assignments require computer software**
   Professors have assigned homework that requires the use of a word processor and the software programs Lotus 1-2-3 and MYSTAT.

2. **Campus computers may not fit student needs**
   Computer facilities on campus are available to students during limited hours, which may not fit into a student's hectic schedule.

   During final exam periods, these computer facilities can become very congested.

   There are many different brands of personal computers on campus. It is difficult and time-consuming to learn how to use them all.

3. **Potential employers seek computer literate applicants**
   It is essential to know how to use a computer in today's business world.

   Purchase of a computer should be seen as part of the cost of education and as a tool in securing employment.

4. **Computer can be used after college education is completed**
   Computers are used regularly in all phases of our lives.

   After college, the computer will not gather dust as some textbooks do.

   Examples of home use include: bookkeeping, office work at home, banking, homework, communications and entertainment.

COST
IBM offers excellent prices for personal computers to UConn students. A computer that fits the student's needs costs $2300. This includes a central processor, color monitor, printer and software. Other companies offer similar systems at costs over $3500.

EXERCISE **27** **Choose one of the following situations and complete it as an oral or written exercise.**

1. Your company has been caught up in an environmental problem (discharging a pollutant, dumping hazardous wastes, discovering asbestos in the office walls, etc.). You have been given responsibility for convincing the people you manage that the problem is under control. Create an argument that begins with a claim, presents evidence and has an explicit rationale.

2. You want to introduce a plan to help teach a large number of illiterate people how to read and write. These employees can perform, but their sense of self-esteem is very low because of their illiteracy. Create a convincing plan based on Toulmin Logic.

3. Your department or group has just been attacked by a client who is dissatisfied with your performance. The CEO asks you, "What are you going to do about this?" Write a letter to the client using Toulmin Logic.

4. You're about to terminate an employee. Let us hear your case against him/her. Use Toulmin Logic (this can be a memo or a dialogue).

19

P R I N C I P L E

Avoid Logical Errors

If something is good (or bad), it's not necessarily the case that its opposite is bad (or good).

Edward De Bono

No discussion on logic can be complete without the mention of logical errors or fallacies. The following list can be helpful, not because you need to memorize it, but because you can use it to find examples in what you read, speak and hear every day. Even more important, you can become a more persuasive advocate if you can point out the logical errors in others' arguments and avoid such errors in your own thinking.

For example, the "either/or" (or "black and white") error is so widespread we hardly recognize it in our own thinking. Statements like "Either you're for or against this," or "They're too young or too old," or "Put up or shut up!" are common examples.

We write because we want to be believed. But if our thinking contains one glaring logical error, we lose credibility. We need to train ourselves to see that either/or is not appropriate thinking; that "both/and" is more accurate in many situations.

1. The Hasty Generalization

    This is the error that occurs most often in inductive reasoning. A hasty generalization is a conclusion reached prematurely without sufficient study of the evidence.

    Example: His past experience as Dogpatch County Chairman makes him the best candidate for the U.S. Senate.

2. The Either/Or Error or False Dilemma

    This error presumes that there are only two ways of looking at a situation — or that only one of two choices can be made when actually other alternatives do exist.

    Example: Either you are for the MX missile, or you are an isolationist.

3. The Unknowable Statistic

    Inductive reasoning requires some knowledge of statistics and how they can be used or misused as evidence. To evaluate whether statistics are used fairly and reliably, you need to look for such things as the **size of the sample**, whether it is **representative** and **random**, and whether a **margin for error** was considered. The error of the unknowable statistic refers to confusion or deception in the use of statistics or to citing figures that would be impossible to obtain.

    Example: Only 106 of an estimated 895 cases of rape in New England last year were reported.

4. Inconsistencies and Contradiction

    Inconsistencies and contradictions appear in both inductive and deductive reasoning. To say "all men are equal, but some are more equal than others" is to reason deductively with two contradictory premises. In this case, one of the premises has to be false.

    Example: Of course, I cannot approve of hecklers disrupting my opponent's speeches. However, I would also say that in a democracy, they also have the right to be heard as much as the speaker.

5. The Loaded Question

    Loaded questions occur often in polls to create a bias toward a certain answer.

Example: Do you believe pornography should be brought into every home through television? Have you stopped beating your wife? Are you still a heavy drinker?

6. The False Analogy

An analogy is a form of reasoning in which two relationships or qualities are compared to one another. A good analogy often compares some abstract principle that is difficult to understand to a concrete, familiar experience in order to make the abstract principle clearer. A good sound analogy must compare two relationships that have major parallels in the aspects under consideration.

In a false analogy, however, important differences that may invalidate the "logic" of the analogy are either overlooked or willfully disregarded.

Example: There is no convincing evidence to show that cigarette smoking is harmful. Too much of anything is harmful. Too much applesauce is harmful.

7. False Cause

An argument that insists on a causal connection between events that cannot reasonably be connected, or interprets causation in an oversimplistic manner without evidence contains this error.

Example: Nasrudin was throwing handfuls of crumbs around his house. "What are you doing?" someone asked.
"Keeping the tigers away."
"But there are no tigers in these parts."
"That's right. Effective, isn't it?"

8. The Slippery Slope

The slippery slope is another causal error. In this case, the claim is made that permitting one event to occur would set off an uncontrollable chain reaction. In politics this is also called the domino theory.

Example: If you offer people unemployment insurance, they will become lazy.

9. Misapplied Generalization

An argument that states a generalization with the insistence that it has no exceptions and should be applied even to atypical situations is guilty of the misapplied generalization.

Example: Milk is good for everybody. You should drink at least a glass a day.

10. Begging the Question

The error of begging the question occurs in an argument in which no argument is really offered in the premises; the conclusion is only asserted and then reasserted, as though it were an explanation. "A is true because A is true."

Example: Beethoven was the greatest composer of all time because he wrote the greatest music.

11. Errors of Ambiguity, Euphemism and Equivocation

Examples: a. We should treat drug use as a private right that harms no one but the user. My mother takes aspirin every day and no one stops her.
b. We haven't locked him up. He's in protective custody.
c. We can't say that we aren't capable of not doing it.

12. Covert Persuasion

Slanted language: emotional appeals to fear, pity, authority, bandwagon mentality, personal attack and "poisoning the well" are all irrational appeals disguised as rational arguments. This does not mean that any argument that includes expression of feeling or emotion is invalid. To be sane on many topics is to feel clear anger, indignation or grief. However, a fallacious argument is not always clear about its feeling involvement.

Example: Next stop — Central America? No one in Washington wants to send America to war. But events in the region could force the President's hand.

13. The Red Herring

The term *red herring* comes from the ruse used by prison escapees of smearing themselves with herring to throw dogs off the scent of their tracks. The red herring in argumentation succeeds in being most distracting when it proves a point other than the one being addressed. Its purpose is to sidetrack opponents into irrelevancies and divert them from the issue at hand.

Example: Marijuana smoking can't be all that bad. I would feel safer any day driving with a marijuana smoker than a driver under the influence of liquor.

14. Poisoning the Well

This error involves creating prejudice or discrediting the point of view of your opponent.

Example: "How can you even think of listening to the tax proposals of a public official who has been sued by his secretary for sexual harassment?"

EXERCISE **28** Identify the following as either 1. Correct, 2. Hasty Generalization, 3. Either/or Error, 4. Unknowable Statistic, 5. False Analogy, 6. False Cause, 7. Slippery Slope, 8. Loaded Question, 9. Inconsistencies and Contradictions:

_____ 1. German and Japanese industry have nothing to teach American industry. Sure, they're both ahead of us in some ways now. But they were also ahead of us in 1942 and look what happened.

_____ 2. All American men love cars.

_____ 3. Deregulation has damaged every American enterprise it has attempted to help. It has been a boondoggle from start to finish. We need to end deregulation.

_____ 4. "There are two sorts of stockholders who oppose this corporation's South African holdings. The first are those who are simply misinformed with respect to our policies, which attempt to weaken apartheid through constructive engagement. The second are those who fear that their dividends will suffer as a result of product boycotts..."

_____ 5. "Militant environmentalists represent a new and frightening stage in the left wing's control of this country's energy policies and resources. If they can block Diablo Canyon Nuclear Plant with impunity, what's to stop them from doing the same thing to coal or gas or oil?"

E X E R C I S E 28
(concluded)

_____ 6. Writing a good essay takes a lot of thinking and planning.

_____ 7. A few years ago, I was able to go on a tour of Chinese industry.

_____ 8. Last year I took a personal finance course and it was boring. Business courses just don't teach you anything useful or interesting.

_____ 9. In 1989 our college increased the math requirement for graduation. In 1990 we had the smallest freshman class in five years. We must abolish the new math requirement.

_____ 10. In April I started wearing a more subdued mascara. Next month I landed a job at Merrill Lynch. It's all due to that mascara.

_____ 11. Just as soldiers never question their officers' orders, so managers should never question the C.E.O.'s advice.

_____ 12. Are you still cheating on your taxes?

_____ 13. Only forty-five of the actual eighty-six cases of insider trading in the N.Y.S.E. were reported this year.

_____ 14. Facing an angry crowd of fishermen bearing dead, oil-soaked shellfish, an Exxon spokesman said, "There has been no mismanagement of the Valdez clean-up. The company has completely restored all of the damaged shoreline in Prince William Sound to acceptable levels of cleanliness."

E X E R C I S E 29 **Label the following items as either 1. Correct, 2. Euphemism Used to Disguise Meaning, 3. Bandwagon, or 4. Poisoning the Well.**

_____ 1. An entry device was used to gain access to the headquarters of the terrorists. Their numbers were neutralized without any casualties for our freedom fighters, resulting in the liberation of the country.

_____ 2. How can you even think of listening to the tax proposals of a public official who has been sued by his secretary for sexual harassment?

_____ 3. All our stockholders agree; John Jones is the *only* choice for new C.E.O.

_____ 4. You should buy a BMW. Don't you want to look successful?

_____ 5. Don't vote for proposition 14. The polls show it will lose 4 to 1.

_____ 6. I've found the ByteWrite computer to be best for word processing.

Label the following as either 1. Correct, 2. Red Herring, 3. Pointing to Another Wrong, 4. Personal Attack, or 5. Emotional Appeals to Fear, Pity or Authority.

_____ 1. You can help these sad and ragged orphans with a small donation or you can turn the page.

_____ 2. "I am perplexed why Mr. Keating has been singled out as some kind of devil. Lincoln Savings is only one of hundreds of S & L's that have suffered from bad investments. Why should we make a scapegoat of one man when so many others are also at fault?"

_____ 3. Taking cocaine isn't all that bad. I'd feel safer driving with someone on cocaine than under the influence of alcohol any day.

_____ 4. Guns are not America's major problem. Cars, cancer and accidents in the home all kill far more people than guns do. It is not guns we should be afraid of, but the effects of poverty, lack of education, and a judicial system that sends criminals and psychopaths back out into the streets.

_____ 5. "Mr. Iacocca is a man who frequently engages his mouth before putting his brain in gear."

20

PRINCIPLE

Apply the Laws of Persuasion

You have my word on it.

Joe Isuzu

Ethos: Old Wine in New Bottles

What makes a written document credible? A written document or speech must have that quality Aristotle called *ethos* to be accepted as true and trustworthy. Roughly translated, that means there is no substitute for the audience's perception that the writer or speaker is an ethical man, an honest person of good character. The attributes that are most important are dynamism, sociability, reliability and personal attractiveness. The individual must have an authoritative manner, good sense and goodwill.

The assumption that persuasion depends on the communicator's credibility has held over in modern theories about attitude change and mass communication.

For example, government agencies take great pains to have their statements to Congress presented by the most acceptable advocate.

In television advertisements, scientific backing is used to sell products, while a background of bookcases filled with the Encyclopedia Britannica suggests that the speaker is an expert.

If Surgeon General Koop said it, it had to be true.

If Gary Hart said it after his fall from grace, it couldn't be true.

Findings of the Yale Program of Research on Communication and Attitude Change

The Yale Program of Research on Communication and Attitude Change conducted over 50 experiments between 1946 and 1961 on communication and persuasion. They defined a stimulus-response model and measured attitude and opinion changes, trying to discover the "laws" of persuasion. Their major conclusion was that *expertise* and *trustworthiness* were extremely important factors. Their other findings were:

1. High-credibility vs. low-credibility sources disappear as factors after four weeks, even though previous opinion change was accomplished more significantly through high-credibility sources. This finding is called the **reverse sleeper** effect.

   Usually the **sleeper effect** occurs when an opinion change in the desired direction takes place some time following exposure rather than right after exposure. However, in time the effects of a persuasive communication tend to wear off.

2. Fear increases conformity up to a point. A low dose of fear is better than a high dose. If there is too much fear, the individual will fail to pay attention to what is said.[13]

---

[13] Since the Yale experiments, other studies have refuted some of the conclusions. For example, Leventhal (1970) found that high-fear appeals were usually more effective than moderate or low-fear appeals. He showed the original researchers, Janis and Feshback (1953), did not follow up the high-fear appeal with enough reassurance. Adapting the suggested recommendations did not seem to eliminate the negative consequences. Defensive avoidance of a fear message may occur when the message leaves a person feeling vulnerable regardless of actions taken to deal with the danger.

3. In terms of structure, the communicator should generally state his or her conclusions explicitly <u>unless</u> the audience is intelligent and sophisticated.

4. Both sides of an issue should be included if it is likely that the audience will be exposed to counter-argument.[14]

5. Persons who have low self-esteem are easily influenced.

6. People who are aggressive toward others and who have psychoneurotic tendencies are difficult to influence. People who are most attached to a group are probably least influenced by communications which conflict with group norms.

7. Active participation in communication (such as role playing or giving a speech) changes opinions in the direction argued more effectively than passive participation. Opinions that people make known to others are harder to change than opinions which people hold privately.

8. Put your strongest arguments first for the uninvolved. Put them last for those who are already interested.

9. Present the view you want remembered last.

The laws of common sense

Is there anything more we can add to this synopsis of Yale's research that could help us deliver persuasive messages? Perhaps we can summarize some principles of common sense. There's just no substitute for:

- having an objectively worthwhile idea, product or proposal
- telling the truth
- knowing what you're talking about
- caring about your subject
- being rational, consistent and focused
- keeping your audience's attention
- understanding when you've said enough.

---

[14] Another twist to the Yale experiment on one-sided or two-sided messages is that two-sided messages produce an introduction effect so that people can argue against a later counterpropaganda message.

Most advertisements are one-sided communications. This strategy is probably most effective when the product is well liked, widely consumed, has few competitors and enjoys local customers.

However, if the audience is well informed about a product and its alternatives, if the product is not widely preferred, or if the audience is likely to be exposed to ads for competitive products, then two-sided rather than one-sided ads are more effective.

Indirection versus brute integrity: two cautionary tales

We have been stressing throughout this text that being simple, clear, straightforward and precise are virtues. We have not minimized the issues of audience or tone of voice, tact and strategy. But many critics of American and Western notions of communication have pointed out the limitations of "laying the cards on the table" (telling the truth in unvarnished terms).

Since you will almost certainly be dealing with an increasingly multi-cultural workforce and global economy, you must be aware of the limitations of "brute integrity," as Pascale and Athos label American business tendencies.[15]

Their thesis is that our "high-noon shoot-out" approach is macho and overly straight, and that devious ambiguity, which is alleged to be *female*, is closer to the indirection used in Japan. The Japanese are more sensitive than Americans to saving face and avoiding premature decisions.

I believe that Americans use business writing to cover themselves more than to communicate; therefore, it is unfair to talk about the clear-cut purposes and objectives of a document without knowing the internal politics of a particular situation. Reading between the lines is a sense that <u>survivors</u> acquire, as witnessed by the example of Bruce, a section head at the Bank of America:

[15] P.B. Pascale and A.G. Athos, *The Art of Japanese Management* (New York, 1981).

Performance Appraisals: Outstanding
Relations with Supervisor: Solid

"So you really think this loan is a sound risk in the face of a recessionary economy?" asks Bob, a staff specialist.

"Yes," answers Bruce.

One Week Later: Memo from the Boss

> Bruce, I think you should sit down with Bob and
> discuss your latest loan.

Bruce has never before received a memo from his boss concerning his relationship with Bob. This is unusual. However, he does not rush to the boss and say, "Hey, did Bob come to see you about my judgment on that last loan?" What he does is research the background on the loan very thoroughly to correct any credibility problem he might have.

Harold Geneen's Style of Management — Fear as a Motivator

In a locked room high atop the Manhattan headquarters of IT&T, fifty executives sit around two long, felt-covered tables.

"John, what have you done about the problem?"

"Well, I called him but I couldn't get him to make a commitment."

"Do you want me to call him?"

"Gosh, that's a good idea. Would you mind?"

"I'd be glad to," says Harold Geneen, "but it will cost you your paycheck."

Pathos: Choosing Emotional Appeals

We have spoken already about fear as an emotional appeal leading to conformity. But what about positive feeling? How does that influence attitudes and behavior? "I like Poo Poo Potato Chips," or "I hate Peaceniks" are statements of simplistic attitudes that are positive and negative.

Research has focused on just this basic division, this summary of our beliefs. And a number of tests have been created to measure feelings, behavioral and physiological indicators of attitudes.

1. Interestingly enough, a person arguing **against** his vested interest is more persuasive than someone arguing **for** his vested interest.

   Why? Probably because that person represents a higher ideal. The positive effect of someone telling you the truth, even though it hurts him, is convincing.

2. Two communicators may both be trusted experts on an issue, but one may be more well liked or more physically attractive:

   In the Richard Nixon and John F. Kennedy debate, Kennedy faced the camera squarely and looked directly into the lens. Nixon shifted his eyes and seldom gazed into the camera. Kennedy clearly established a better rapport with his audience.

   Your reader or your listener will accept your beliefs, opinions, conclusions more readily if you are perceived as likeable, familiar and similar (studies by Byrne, 1971; Rokeach, 1960; Berscheid and Walster, 1974; and Sherif and Sherif, 1953).

3. We've spent a great deal of energy learning to argue rationally by using evidence and rationales, so the question arises as to when to use emotional appeals and when to use factual ones. The answer is that it depends on the kind of message and the kind of audience.

   Generally, we would use a rational appeal if we were trying to show our audience how to make money or save money. If we were selling automobile tires, we would talk factually about durability, grip and safety. If we were selling cosmetics, we might appeal to the emotions, to love of beauty, excitement, pleasure, etc.

Surprisingly, there have been few definitive studies about this question, and few conclusive answers. Another surprise is that one of the few things learned suggests that humor is often **not** an effective persuasive technique.

So what have we learned from the ancients and the moderns about persuasion? Most of it boils down to common sense. Whether you're writing a request or a collection letter, a proposal or a recommendation, an advertisement or an option memo you should:

- Know your audience and adjust your argument to suit it
- Use a combination of *logos, ethos and pathos*
- Be confident
- Be enthusiastic
- Be clear and brief.

EXERCISE **30** **Examine the following advertising slogans. Decide on a scale of 1 to 5 which are the most effective. Why? Which ones contain logical errors? What are they?**

1. Better safe than sorry! The Northern Insurance Company.

   Less effective |—1—2—3—4—5—| More effective

   Why?

   Logical error?

2. Lexus! You'll either own one or want one.

   Less effective |—1—2—3—4—5—| More effective

   Why?

   Logical error?

3. It's a fact that people use only 10% of their brain capacity. MetaThink can increase your brain power by 20%.

   Less effective |—1—2—3—4—5—| More effective

   Why?

   Logical error?

4. Give your child a head start with a personal computer by I.B.M.

   Less effective |—1—2—3—4—5—| More effective

   Why?

   Logical error?

EXERCISE **30**
(concluded)

5. There's a reason the competition can't keep up with us. We're just too fast. AT&T.

Less effective |——1——2——3——4——5——| More effective

Why?

Logical error?

EXERCISE **31**

Choose one of the situations below and follow the instructions. In all cases, you should be aware of the difference between persuasion based on reason versus emotion.

1. Study an advertisement or fund-raising letter, an editorial or brochure that illustrates the use of emotional appeals. Test them for *ethos* and identify the *pathos* in the exact emotional appeal.

2. You know from what's being said three levels up that the perception of your department is negative. How do you correct this perception?

3. You're speaking to the retirees of your corporation, trying to persuade them to give more money to the United Way this year.

4. The Environmental Protection Agency has repeatedly pointed out that disposable diapers are not really "disposable," and legislation is now under consideration to ban such products.

   The State Commissioner of Environmental Affairs has pointed out that such legislation poses a serious problem, given the severe shortage of water that plagues your region. Local bans on water use virtually prohibit returning to washable diapers.

   The Commissioner has asked you to provide a response that convincingly opposes the legislation to ban disposable diapers.

5. You have been working at OldBoy Corporation for several years in marketing. Your boss, Mr. Chauvin, discusses with you and another manager, Joe Bloe, the question of who should be the new Director of Planning.

   Joe suggests Mike Ladd, and you suggest Michelle Curry, who has been doing the job anyway as interim Director. Your boss doesn't know who she is? "Why don't I know her?" he asks.

Scene: The Board Room

Several men are chatting before the meeting begins. Michelle comes into the room in navy blue suit, white blouse. She glances at the men, who go on chatting. She passes by them and sits down at the conference table.

Mr. Chauvin enters and sits at the head of the table. Michelle is on his left. You are at the end of the table. There are several other managers present.

The boss asks how everyone is going to handle the problem of increased marketing responsibilities. Michelle says quietly, "I think we're going to have to increase staffing, at least clerical staffing. There's no way we can do the work without more support positions."

Mr. Chauvin ignores her as several other managers speak about the need for conceptualizers and the possibilities of convincing the CEO, Mr. Oldboy, that this is the time to expand upper level marketing positions, bringing on board more talent. They mention the names of several people they know working in other companies.

Michelle looks frustrated. "I think it's a mistake to push for upper level positions in the present…" She is interrupted in mid-sentence by the man on her left.

You notice that the boss ignores everything she says. It's as though she doesn't exist. What should you do?

6. Your organization, Contact Utilities, has just received the following letter:

> "Your trucks have been on my front lawn and have created deep ruts in my property. I know there is an easement to allow you to dig up your pipeline, but I am upset that you have ruined my entire front lawn. I insist that you do something about this as soon as possible."

How would you answer the customer? What would be the components of your letter? Is it a persuasive letter? Assume that you want to keep the letter writer a satisfied customer.

21

P R I N C I P L E

Avoid Using Propaganda

What is the difference between persuasion and propaganda? Both of them appeal to reason and emotion, but there are distinctions that we all recognize. Persuasion can border on propaganda when we tell only one side of the story (a technique called "card stacking").

Even using testimonials or high-credibility sources can smack of propaganda if the intent is to cover an inadequate person or product with a borrowed cloak of respectability. Although the distinctions aren't always clear-cut, persuasion **encourages** thought whereas propaganda **manipulates** thought, tending towards deception or distortion.

Persuasion uses the ancient approaches of Aristotle: *ethos*, *pathos* and *logos*. Propaganda sells snake oil, pressures you, hints at wrongdoing or waves the flag. Propaganda also manipulates public opinion for purposes that are not in the public's best interest.

Here are a few of the techniques that can be labeled propaganda:

1. Name Calling
Derogatory term to create a negative emotional attitude for an individual or thing.

   You don't want a polluting, gas-guzzling Smogmobile! Buy a clean, solar-powered SunCycle instead!

2. Card Stacking
Telling the facts for one side only.

   This method of staff reduction cuts operating costs; reduces insurance, pension, and other long-range costs, and provides for easier staff training and supervision. [The firing of 60 teachers and doubling of classes is not mentioned.]

3. Testimonials
Using someone's testimony to persuade you to think as they do.

   I never believed there was much difference in hair color products till I tried HALO. My hair never looked so shimmery. For shimmery hair I will always use HALO.

4. Prestige Identification
Using a well-known figure to lend importance or prestige to a product.

   The football star who sells Pigskins junk food, or the President's brother who endorses Billy-Bob beer.

5. Bandwagon
Using the argument that everyone's doing it, so you should too.

   Join the millions of Americans who are switching to Burpsi Cola! In taste tests, 104% of the participants preferred Burpsi, the choice of an entire generation.

6. Exigency
Creating the impression that your action is required immediately or an opportunity will be lost forever.

   For a short time only, this limited edition of Norwegian carpenters' songs is being offered at rock-bottom prices. Don't wait another minute. Order yours now, before supplies are depleted. Not available in stores.

7. Transfer
   Attempting to have you transfer your feelings about something you value to a different product or service.

   Make your home a showplace. Get Neva-Stayn vinyl slipcovers today and be the envy of the neighborhood.

8. Innuendo
   Hinting that someone is hiding something.

   Unlike his opponent, Senator Slugwell failed to undergo voluntary drug testing before the primary.

9. Snob Appeal
   Trying to persuade by making you feel you are one of the elite if you use brand X or Y.

   Live a legend of elegance with Linnet china and crystal. Limited edition available to club members only.

10. Flag Waving
    Connecting the use of a product with patriotism.

    Blitzer cars are better than Japanese cars. Good old American know-how goes into each Blitzer product, and they're the cheapest cars in the world with a driver's sick-bag. Advantage BLITZER!

EXERCISE **32** **Choose one of the situations below and follow the instructions.**

1. Identify a situation in which you have used propaganda. Now put yourself into the shoes of the person(s) receiving your message. How do you feel?

2. Think of an incident in which you've fallen for propaganda. Tell us in a one-page letter what you learned about gullibility quotient.

3. You are members of the Board of Directors of the Baseball Hall of Fame. You have been summoned to a special meeting to consider the case of Pete Rose. The Baseball Commissioner has disciplined Rose for his gambling, and Rose has also been convicted of federal income tax evasion.

   You must decide whether Pete Rose should be eligible for election to Baseball's Hall of Fame, given that he is the all-time greatest hitter in the history of the game. You must also decide how best to communicate your decision.

   Choose an argument using propaganda, then choose one using *ethos* and *logos*. Which is more effective?

4. Sell a perfume, a house in the "right" neighborhood, or membership in a private club by designing a brochure. Use propaganda to tell the truth, but not the whole truth.

5. Write a 30-second TV or radio commercial for any product of service, real or imaginary. First, use what you consider to be propaganda appeal. Then use a legitimate emotional appeal. Which is more effective?

22

P R I N C I P L E

Use Creative Thinking by Going beyond Rational Thought

Imagination is more important than knowledge.

Albert Einstein

We can never have full information about the future, and yet our actions now will have future consequences. Therefore, creative thinking is the best way we have of generating alternatives for consideration. Designing strategies, contingencies and fall-back situations are all part of a creative design process.

Information and logical thinking set the framework, but creative design offers the possibilities. After exploring the possibilities, we then turn to logic to assess their validity. Instead of striving to be right, it is more important to be flexible and open. Fortunately, business mentalities are moving in this direction. Proactive thinking is the password and proactive thinking requires creativity. Creative thinking takes many forms and covers a wide range of different skills. One approach is embodied in the concept of "divergent thinking."

Corollaries for Divergent Thinking:

- Turn off your left brain
- Brainstorm with others
- Turn off your "critic"
- Go beyond yes and no
- Defer judgment
- Turn on your right brain
- Use free association
- Create a mess, then sort it out
- Force relationships
- Seek combinations

Much creative thinking and writing begins when internal criticism is suspended, and the mind plays somewhere between conscious and unconscious thought. Imagine yourself swinging between earth and sky, your mind completely open. You tip backwards. You see what's below you from an upside-down vantage point. Your consciousness changes. Our purpose is to come up with something new, a discovery, a fresh combination of ideas that fulfills a need, an original approach, perhaps a *eureka* experience.

Sometimes this happens by creating a system to explain a process or concept, as Freud and Darwin did. Sometimes we relate new information to prior knowledge and we come up with a synthesis, like Robert Noyce creating the first integrated circuit.

Consider the case of August Kekulé, who discovered the elusive shape of the benzene ring after dreaming of a snake that devoured its own tail. Or rocket pioneer Robert Goddard, who climbed apple trees as a boy and gazed at the stars. Or Einstein, whose contributions to the theories of Coriolis motion came to him as he watched swirling tea leaves in a stirred cup.

Follow the Rules for Brainstorming

In Alex Osborn's book *Applied Imagination*, he summarizes one way to find new ideas. Osborn's pioneering use of brainstorming and problem-solving techniques hinges on a list of "idea-spurring" questions and strategies:

1. Do not criticize or judge. All ideas are acceptable.

2. Free-wheel. The offbeat and impractical may lead to practical breakthroughs.

3. Aim for quantity. The more ideas produced, the more chances there are for solutions. It is important to get the obvious ideas "out of the system" because they can block production of new ideas.

4. Piggy-back or hitch-hike. It's OK to build on others' ideas. This process can involve the SCAMPER steps listed below:

S UBSTITUTE: What could you substitute? What might you do instead? What would do as well or better?

C OMBINE: What could you combine? What might work well together? What could be brought together?

A DAPT: What could be adjusted to suit a purpose or condition? How could you make it fit?

M ODIFY: What would happen if you changed form or quality?

MAGNIFY: Could you make it larger, greater or stronger?

MINIFY: Could you make it smaller, lighter or slower?

P UT TO OTHER USES: Could you use it for another purpose? What are new ways to apply it? What does it suggest?

E LIMINATE: What could you subtract or take away?

R EVERSE: REARRANGE: What would happen if you reversed or flipped it? Could you change the parts, layout or sequence?

A similar list was created by John Arnold for his Creative Engineering course at M.I.T.:[16]

Can we increase the **function**? Can we make the product do more things?

Can we get a **higher performance level**? Make the product longer lived? More reliable? More accurate? Safer? More convenient to use? Easier to repair and maintain?

Can we lower the **cost**? Eliminate excess parts? Substitute cheaper materials? Design to reduce hand labor or for complete automation?

Can we increase the **salability**? Improve the appearance of the product? Improve the package? Improve its point of sale?

[16] James L. Adams, *Conceptual Blocking: A Guild to Better Ideas* (New York, 1974).

Now, here are a couple of charts that show how lists like Osborn's and Arnold's can lead to the improvement of a simple camera or a new method of collecting tolls:

Component Part	Attributes and Specifications	Ideas Generated
Camera Body	Weight?	Wafer-size and shape. Imitation of clothing or accessories. Expansion size.
Lens	Size?	All-in-one. Interchangeable, built-in filters. Automatic lens. Expansion hood.
Film	Shape? Color?	Interchangeable pre-loaded camera backs. Multi-type, dial yourself film.
Viewfinder	Material?	Periscope. Bright, contrasting colors for focus.
Strap	Flexibility?	Multiple length. Variable functions: wrist, arm, neck.

Component Part	Attributes and Limitations	Ideas Generated
Toll Station	Straight booths. Small coin slot slows traffic.	Exact change. Diagonal booths. Double-decker booths. Half-mile grating in road to drop coins.
Toll Collector	Reluctant to lean out booth. Human error in making change.	Robot collector. Basket. Coded cards. Stickers. Eliminate toll (tax cars). Collect only 1 way. Camera surveillance.
Traffic Variety	Time needed to process buses and trucks slows	No tolls for fully loaded cars and buses. Truck and bus lanes. Special time for large vehicles.
Traffic Merging after toll	Congestion and accidents, especially in bad weather.	Lengthen distance of the merge. Install tracks to control merge. Timed lights. No merge.

EXERCISE **33** **Let's try to apply some of these approaches to the following problems or opportunities:**

1. Invent new uses for the paper cup. Brainstorm with a group. Go around until the associations become non-rational, surprising, imaginative, far-fetched.

2. Design a new toothbrush that will either save time or be more effective. What about a new bicycle seat? A new beach chair? A new shoe?

3. Create a list of things that bother you. Now choose one item from that list and brainstorm an invention or solution. Be very specific.

   EXAMPLE:

   Things that bother me

   - rotten oranges
   - broken shoe laces
   - bumper stickers
   - doors that stick

   Brainstorm on rotten oranges

   - smelly in refrigerator
   - use tupperware
   - use baking soda
   - detector that renews baking soda when oranges go bad

4. Choose a group of 6 – 10 people. Choose a notekeeper and a chairperson. Define a problem and brainstorm a number of solutions. The notekeeper will report the best solutions back to the full group.

   Brainstorming shouldn't go on too long (20–25 minutes should be time enough to generate new ideas). There should be a notetaker and a facilitator to ensure that no one monopolizes the process. The facilitator also should:

   - start and stop the session
   - make sure people stop "evaluating" ideas
   - make suggestions when the ideas dry up
   - ensure that a spectrum of approaches is tried.

5. Within the session, try to force a relationship or find a new combination.

   Example of a forced relationship: Design a new space suit. Stare at the ceiling. What thoughts occur? Can you apply these thoughts to the problem? What fabrics would you use? What qualities would you seek?

6. Look at the following graphic and the table of contents below it. Create an executive summary about the purpose, description and market for a "Drawing Room" business in the city of your choice (New York, Los Angeles, Chicago, etc.).

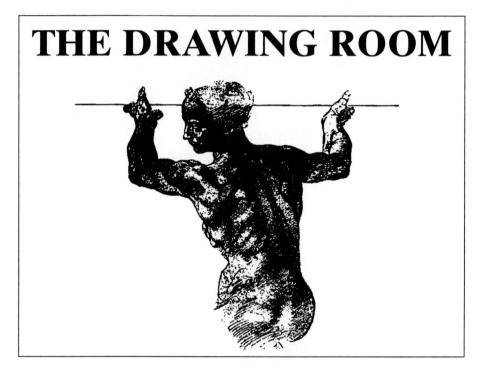

THE DRAWING ROOM

Table of Contents

A. Statement of Purpose
B. Description of the Business
C. The Market
D. Competition
E. Management & Personnel
F. Financial Data
G. Appendices
　　1. Three Year Income Summary
　　2. First Year Operations Statement
　　3. Supporting Schedules

Edward De Bono's System to Encourage Creative Thinking

Edward De Bono is credited with coining the term "lateral thinking," which occurs when the mind interrupts its habitual, organized (vertical) thought processes and leaps sideways out of ingrained patterns. He is regarded as a leading international authority in the field of conceptual thinking and has been hired by a number of Fortune 500 companies to help their key executives become more productive.

His model of the brain and how it works is not mechanistic. Instead, he sees the brain as a pan of jelly. As drops of hot water fall on the jelly, they make imprints. The hot water comes from outside (the stimulus of the environment, sensory input). Various patterns form: perceptual, linguistic, social and muscular. We can't "think" ourselves out of these patterns. In fact, we don't control them at all; they control us. Only by changing perceptions can we change those patterns. De Bono provides a highly structured method of provocation that forces you to move **across** patterns to find a new approach.

> **Example:** We are accustomed to think of rivers as always going downstream. Factories traditionally draw in clean water from upstream and dump their wastes downstream. What if they were required to <u>reverse</u> this and draw in their water downstream from their outlet pipes? If they had to receive what they dump, they might be more interested in solving the pollution problem.[17]

"PO" is De Bono's expression for breaking down the established patterns to introduce discontinuity. YES/NO is the basic tool of logical thinking. *The old pattern of YES/NO leads to polarizations and sharp, artificial differences.* We see black or white, friend or foe. We end up with neat, simplistic boxes filled with neat, simplistic ideas. Language often may require such definitions, but creative thinking does not need them.

> **Example:** Prison can provide the freedom to create. Eldridge Cleaver wrote *Soul on Ice* in prison. Nelson Mandela inspired his people and the world from prison. Alexander Solzhenitzyn began *Ivan Denizovitch* while still in the gulag.

In the YES/NO system, we proceed from one certainty to the next. We must be right at every step. If I am right and we disagree, then you

[17] Edward De bono, *Mechanics of the Mind*, p. 143.

must be wrong. If I believe that nudity is wrong, then Polynesian women should be made to wear bras, and Michelangelo's "David" should wear a fig leaf.

In the YES/NO system, the world is divided into separate objects. These objects are either similar or not similar. They are either there or not there. From this division, we arrive at the principle of identity or non-identity that underlies most rational logic. You cannot "be" and "not-be" at the same time. You can't jump and not-jump out of the path of a car. PO, on the other hand, is the word for creative thought that precedes action. You can imagine yourself walking through fire. You can picture the heat and smoke and danger. And then you can create a fire-resistant suit. But you can't walk through the fire and design the suit at the same time.

Traditionally, we've been concerned only with the thinking that comes <u>after</u> perception. Now let's focus on those earlier glimmerings, intuitive flashes that occur in the dark part of our minds where the jelly is not yet deeply patterned.

Lateral thinking, according to De Bono, is closely related to insight, creativity and humor. The difference is that De Bono makes it a more deliberate process. The basic nature of lateral thinking is that:

1. it changes patterns
2. it is an attitude and method of using information
3. it is not a judgment
4. it is a provocation
5. it is a refusal to accept assumptions
6. it is an attempt to escape from "concept" prisons.

When do we use it? When we are stuck and the "old" way is not working. Yes! But also when the question of right or wrong does not arise. What are the differences between lateral and vertical thinking? And when should we switch to the former?

1. Vertical thinking is selective; lateral thinking is generative.

   Rightness matters in vertical thinking. Recklessness matters in lateral thinking. With vertical thinking, you select the most promising approach. With lateral thinking, you generate as many alternative approaches as possible.

2. Vertical thinking moves if there is a direction to move in. Lateral thinking moves to generate a direction.

   The vertical thinker says, "I know what I'm looking for." The lateral thinker says, "I won't know what I'm looking for until I've found it."

3. Vertical thinking is analytic; lateral thinking is provocative.

   Statement: That person is a hypocrite.

   Responses: a. You are wrong.
   b. Interesting. How do you reach that conclusion?
   c. Very well. What happens next? How will you go forward with that idea?

4. Vertical thinking is sequential.

$$A — B — C — D$$

5. Lateral thinking can make jumps.

6. With vertical thinking, one has to be correct at every step; with lateral thinking, one does not.

   There are times when you may have to be wrong to be right at the end.

7. With vertical thinking, you concentrate and exclude what is irrelevant; with lateral thinking you welcome chance intrusions.

8. With vertical thinking, classifications, categories and labels are fixed; with lateral thinking, they are not.

9. Vertical thinking follows the most likely paths; lateral thinking explores the least likely.

10. Vertical thinking is a finite process; lateral thinking is a probabilistic one.

EXERCISE **34** **Choose one of the following situations and "solve" it using lateral thinking. Remember, <u>creativity</u> is essential to solving all of these problems.**

1. A man walks into a bar and asks for a glass of water. The girl behind the bar suddenly pulls out a gun and shoots him. Why?

2. A man owes money to a mean, vicious money lender. The money lender proposes to cancel the debt if he can marry the man's beautiful young daughter. The money lender says, "I will put two stones in this bag. Your daughter must choose a stone. If she chooses the white one, you can keep the money. If she chooses the black one, she must marry me. If she refuses to choose, you will go to jail for debt."

   The daughter sees the money lender place 2 black stones in the bag. What can she do?

3. Imagine yourself as an animal. Get up and move around the room as that animal. Make noises. Now think of yourself as another animal. Go through the same process. Draw a picture of yourself as those two animals combined. What are the qualities of your combination? Do you have those qualities in you? In what managerial situation would you use them? Describe it.

4. Choose two words that have no apparent relationship and brainstorm until you find a connection.

5. You are working for the telephone company, which makes more money based on the **number** of calls placed rather than the **length** of those calls. People in your region tend to use pay phones for lengthy local calls. Design a phone that will discourage endless conversations.

6. There is a shortage of fresh water in Southern California. What system can you invent to solve this problem? (For instance, pipe water down from the glaciers of Alaska.)

7. Most people "go to work" by traveling to a factory, office, school, etc., or by working at home. Can you think of other possibilities?

8. Create a way of handling the problem of speeding drivers.

9. Find new solutions to "burn out" either in the college classroom or on the job.

10. Invent a new computer stand.

11. Reverse some normal "direction" to create a provocation.
    Example: the more money you make for a company, the higher you rise.

12. Create a "stratal" (De Bono's term for a sensitizing technique). Put together five unconnected statements and see if a new idea emerges.

    Example: a "stratal" on car insurance:

    • open to fraud by claimants and repair shops
    • rising costs
    • state regulators and premium caps
    • increasing legal costs
    • differing behavior of selected groups.

PRINCIPLES OF

1994 AND BEYOND

23

P R I N C I P L E

Master Inter-Cultural Communication

Forgive him, for he is a barbarian and thinks that the customs of his tribe are the laws of nature.

George Bernard Shaw

We have been focusing on communication that is essentially American. But by the year 2000, experts have predicted that multinational corporations will control approximately half the world's assets. You will be entering a culturally diverse workforce and a highly complex global work environment. The straightforward, American communication style should be tempered by the increasingly varied audience you will be writing or speaking to.

The purpose of this chapter is to alert you to the growing complexity of the business environment, and prepare you for the challenge of communicating with people who are from different countries and cultures.

In *The Global Negotiation*, T.J. Griffin and W.R. Daggatt suggest that people are essentially the same, but cultures are not. Cultural differences create gulfs, and bridges must be built to span them. These bridges are the relationships that must be formed before any business can take place.

The authors claim that while Americans like to "do deals," we don't build relationships easily. They believe that Americans don't engage readily in what they term "phatic" communication, in other words, small talk or "getting to know you so I can trust you" conversation. Perhaps it is our very emphasis on getting to the point, being efficient, direct, straightforward and logical that makes us impatient with what we consider to be wasting time. We want just the facts. This can cause us to be seen, in some eyes, as tactless and aggressive — well-meaning, perhaps, but too materialistic.

It depends, of course, on who is talking to whom. While we may share some cultural assumptions with some nations and peoples, we must also acknowledge that there are marked differences with others in such concepts as:

1. personal space
2. time
3. context
4. non-verbal communication
5. trust
6. protocol, manners and face-saving
7. decision-making, negotiations and deadlines
8. negative messages
9. emotion and silence.

Space

In some cultures, a distance of a few inches may be comfortable for normal conversation. In others, the same distance may be reserved only for intimate or hostile encounters:

Carlos, a Latino businessman, found it difficult to carry on a comfortable conversation with British entrepreneur Henry. Though he knew of some differences, Carlos did not expect Henry to act so rudely, as if they didn't know each other at all. Henry remained at an extreme, impersonal distance from Carlos. How could they discuss business with Henry sitting across the room behind a big mahogany desk? Carlos felt the business relationship would never work. It was clear to him that Henry had no interest in getting to know his business partners, and this was important to Carlos.

Because Henry is most comfortable doing business at a distance of a few feet and Carlos works within a close physical distance to his colleagues, the negotiation was ineffective simply because of space preferences. Large distances between people are rare in Latin America —

even in public areas where strangers stand inches from each other quite comfortably.

Henry would feel his personal space was violated if Carlos worked as closely to him as he normally would to his Latin American colleagues. Knowing these "comfort zones" can help you understand that your counterpart isn't trying to intimidate you by standing close. It is only natural and comfortable for some cultures. If Carlos and Henry had known more about each other's sense of personal space, the meeting would have been more successful. Before you travel abroad on business, make note of each culture's business and personal distances.

Time

Edward T. Hall characterizes different cultures as ***monochronic*** or ***polychronic***. Different cultures and peoples normally display varying degrees of these two characteristics:

Monochronic People	Polychronic People
Do one thing at a time	Do many things at once
Concentrate on the task at hand	Are highly distractable
Are "low context"	Are "high context"
Commit to the job	Commit to people and relationships
Adhere to plans	Change plans often and easily
Work within short-term relationships	Tend to build lifetime relationships
Take time commitments seriously	View time commitments as sensible goal
Emphasize promptness	Base promptness on each relationship

Try to place some of the cultures you are more familiar with in one of the two categories. Where would you expect to find Americans? Japanese? Germans? Arabs? French?

If you said Americans and Germans are *monochronic*, you are right. Japanese and Arabs are *polychronic* people. The Spanish are more difficult to classify, but possess more polychronic than monochronic characteristics. Time is regarded so differently among people from different cultures that it is perhaps the most frustrating change for many business people to overcome.

Context

Context is a third major aspect of cultural difference. Edward Hall classifies **high-context** cultures as those in which most of the information is contained within the senders and receivers of that information. Less of it is in the explicit message. **Low-context** cultures would be the opposite, such as the German culture, which prefers everything spelled out in detail; there must be no ambiguity in business transactions. The Japanese, by contrast, say more with less. Because there are only 50 sounds in the language, spoken Japanese can often be vague. Therefore, the finer meanings of conversation are largely context-driven. It is not enough to know the language; unless you also grasp the cultural context, you may miss the subtleties of meaning that can make or break a business deal.

Of all the high-context cultures, Chinese is the highest. When asked something that seems odd, the Chinese will reply to the question that *should have been asked*, giving an answer that may have no relation to the actual question that was asked:

During negotiations, some Americans asked the Chinese, "Do you have access to a small computer?" They meant and should have asked, "Do you have a computer in your facility so that you can do this software development?" The Chinese answered "yes," but the nearest computer they had "access" to was over 50 miles away. It was impossible for them to develop the software, yet the contract was signed. In the end, the American company had to give them $30,000 worth of computer hardware and software for free.

Context can be illustrated as a kind of continuum, with each culture placed between high and low:

High-Context Cultures

Chinese
Japanese
Arab
Greek
Spanish
Italian
English
French
American
Scandinavian
German
German-Swiss

Low-Context Cultures

Non-Verbal Communication

Differences in non-verbal communication are sometimes subtle. But the truth is that we are surrounded by a giddy montage of vivid gestures. People all over the world use their hands, heads and bodies to communicate. It has been estimated that from 60% to 95% of **all** our communication is non-verbal.

In *Gestures: The Do's and Taboos of Body Language Around the World,* Roger E. Axtell gives us a thorough account of the uses of body language in different cultures. The Japanese bow, for example, is not an act of subservience, but a symbol of respect and humility. While Americans pride themselves on a firm handshake, to the Japanese this can seem aggressive and impolite. In Brazil, our "OK" gesture (made with thumb and index finger in a circle) is considered quite rude.

Or consider the visiting American politician whose slightly offset V-for-Victory sign was interpreted by his Australian hosts as insulting. That sign, when flashed with the palm inward, is equivalent in Australia to our rude middle-finger gesture.

According to Axtell, there is only **one** universal "gesture" that runs no risk of misinterpretation: the smile. It is necessary, therefore, before you travel to another country, to ask yourself a number of questions about non-verbal communication:

1. What are the gestures used in your host country for greetings, good-byes, emphasis, friendliness, etc?
2. Should you make eye contact with people you're talking to?
3. Whom should you touch or not touch? How often should you touch?
4. How will the clothes or jewelry of this culture affect your opinion of the people? How will yours affect them?
5. Will you be offended by certain odors? Will, say, the cologne or perfume you use be offensive to others?
6. How fast, slow, loud, soft, monotonously or expressively do your hosts speak?
7. What other cultural assumptions will you have to rethink?

A group of Greek businessmen traveled to Saudi Arabia to negotiate with some Arab emirs. Throughout the negotiations, the Arabs wore sunglasses. This made the Greeks quite uncomfortable. Not only did they fail to maintain a good bargaining position, they felt they were unable to communicate effectively. The Greeks ultimately failed to secure what they felt to be the best results from their negotiation.

To the Arabs, the *eyes* are the windows to the mind. Arabs are experts at understanding people through eye contact. They feel they maintain a better bargaining position when they wear dark glasses because their counterpart is unable to see what they are thinking. They, however, can see what the other is thinking, and therefore have the advantage. Greeks, North Americans and Latin Americans prefer a high degree of eye contact and often feel that Arabs are "untrustworthy" when they cannot see their eyes.

These suggestions do not cover all non-verbal influences on business communication. Frequently, the **unexpected** should have been anticipated:

A major U.S. pharmaceutical company launched a multi-million dollar advertising campaign for its new pain killer, using green as the primary layout color. Unfortunately, the market it was breaking into equated green with disease. The drug did not sell.

The advertising campaign did not communicate healing; it communicated disease. Obviously such things as color, sex, and image can influence business effectiveness, both positively and negatively.

Trust

Trust is a vital part of any business negotiation. It comes sometimes after patient negotiations and a lengthy relationship. However, **first impressions are extremely important**. In China, for instance, gift-giving is a highly regarded, symbolic gesture used to establish trust in new business ventures:

A representative from a large American insurance agency was sent to China to establish relations for expansion in that market. He was told to find a symbolic gift for the businessman he planned to meet. After looking at numerous options and learning how the Chinese interpret certain items and colors, he selected a crystal calyx (the bud of a new flower) to symbolize their budding relationship.

This is an example of how trust can be established in one country. It is different in others. In China, courtesy and respect are valued, and gift-giving is an important aspect of that. Although establishing trust is different in each relationship, it is an integral part of success in all international business ventures.

Protocol, Manners and Face-Saving

Anyone who thinks protocol isn't important is wasting an opportunity to succeed. For the most part, protocol translates into formality regarding rank, and status. But it also involves concepts of manners, rituals, expectations and forms.

In India, for example, academic rank falls just after top political titles. A professor is "superior" to a physician. Entire title pyramids are used in correspondence or on business cards to signify the relative importance of the individual.

In Japan's early history, a serious disregard for manners could be punishable by death. The Japanese were required to behave in precisely prescribed ways. Even today, codes of conduct play a significant role in Japanese lives. More important than the accomplishment of a task is the question of how one goes about the task: does he act sincerely, for example? More important than expertise is how one gets along with others. More important than profits is harmony.

In contrast, Westerners are more concerned with the principle of **things**, of hard "measures" and objective facts. We are goal-oriented. We say "a good loser is still a loser," or "nice guys finish last." To many cultures, this borders on the boorish.

Another concept that varies from culture to culture is that of "face." While face-saving is highly significant in China and Japan, it is also important everywhere. What an American may see as honest and constructive criticism might feel like a blow to pride and dignity in other cultures.

EXERCISE **35** **Discuss the following situations and decide whether there has been a breach of protocol or manners, or if there is a loss of face.**

1. Sue, a recent M.B.A. from The University of Connecticut, has a management position in an international accounting firm. She has been with the company less than a year, but because she is a star performer and is fluent in German, she has been given a job in Germany. The German accountants have been with the company for a number of years. Sue is 30 years old. She finds that no matter what she does, the group she is supposed to supervise won't listen to her.

2. An American representing Merck in Europe and the Middle East has just arrived from Paris where he has mastered the act of kissing the wives of his French hosts on both cheeks. He shakes hands with his new Arab host, only to encounter a soft, lingering handshake, which he draws away from. The wife of his host greets him, and he leans politely forward to kiss her on the cheek.

3. In China, an American businesswoman visits a factory and is met by workers who clap their hands. With a big smile, the American joins in the applause.

4. An American businessman arrives at the home of his Indian host 30 minutes after the agreed-on hour. He brings a box of golf balls as a sign of friendship and is asked by his host to begin the meal. He refuses twice and only after the third request does he start to eat.

EXERCISE **35**
(concluded)

5. An American executive arrives in Russia for an appointment with a newly-formed Russian export company. He wants to get down to business immediately and catch the earliest flight for Germany. Instead, he is asked to wait in his hotel room for an hour and then join the Russians for dinner and the theater. The next day, he is given a tour of Moscow. He is very upset and impatient, and feels that the Russians are just sizing him up.

Decision Making, Negotiations and Deadlines

We cannot begin to summarize all the guidelines for successful global negotiations. But it is important to emphasize that **patience and flexibility** will go a long way in building the positive connections you want.

The following anecdote illustrates why you must always be alert to the unexpected and able to deal with it under trying circumstances:

Two Sikorsky Aircraft executives went to Turkey to sell helicopters. They found themselves in the same room with their French competitors. The Turks began the negotiations by asking the French and Americans to begin bidding against each other. After a week of this "auction" in a room thick with cigarette smoke, the French could not go on without calling home to discuss their offer with their superiors.

All the rules that had been hammered out were suspended, and the bargaining began again from scratch. Finally, the two competitors were asked to submit their lowest bids in sealed envelopes. The translator for the Americans said, "You're not going to like this, but they want you to start over again." Both the Americans and the French refused, and the Turks then picked Sikorsky's bid.

Perhaps the negotiators should have been aware of the Turkish proverb that states, "Ask much, but take as much as they offer."

Remember that "giving face" is just as important as "saving face." You should allow a competing negotiator to achieve a result that is consistent with his or her principles or previous statements or actions.[18]

[18] Trenholme Griffin, *The Global Negotiator*, pp.96–98.

The tables on the next two pages summarize some stereotypical styles of persuasion used by negotiators in different cultures. They will not be true in every case.

Table 1

Cultural Styles of Persuasion[19]

	North Americans North Europeans	Arabs Latin Americans	Russians
Primary Negotiating Style and Practice	Factual: Appeals made to logic	Affective: Appeals made to emotion	Axiomatic: Appeals made to ideals
Opponent's Arguments Countered with...	Objective facts	Subjective feelings	Asserted ideals
Concession Making	Small concessions made early to establish relationship	Concessions made throughout as bargaining process	Few, if any, small concessions made
Response to Opponent's Concessions	Usually reciprocate concessions	Almost always reciprocate concessions	Concessions equal weakness. Rarely reciprocated
Initial Position	Short term	Long term	No continuing relationship
Relationship	Moderate	Extreme	Extreme
Deadlines	Very important	Casual	Ignored

---

[19] Source: Glenn, Witmeyer, and Stevenson, "Cultural Styles of Persuasion," *International Journal of Intercultural Studies*, volume 1.

Table 2

A Cross-Cultural Perspective of Negotiation Styles[20]

North American	Latin American	Japanese
Emotional sensitivity not highly valued.	Emotional sensitivity valued.	Emotional sensitivity highly valued.
Straightforward or impersonal dealing.	Emotionally passionate.	Hiding of emotions.
Litigation not as much as conciliation.	Great power plays; use of weakness.	Subtle power plays; conciliation.
Lack of commitment to employer/employee.	Loyalty to employer/employee.	Loyalty to employer/employee.
Teamwork provides input to a decision maker.	Decisions come down from one individual.	Group decision consensus.
Decisions made on a cost benefit basis. Face-saving does not always matter.	Face-saving crucial in decision making to preserve honor and dignity.	Face-saving crucial; decisions often made on basis of saving someone from embarrassment.
Decision maker influenced by special interests but often not seen as ethical.	Execution of special interests of decision maker expected and condoned.	Decision makers openly influenced by special interests.
Argumentative when right or wrong, but impersonal.	Passionately argumentative when right or wrong.	Not argumentative; quiet when right.
Great importance given to documentation as evidential proof.	Impatient with documentation as obstacle to understanding general principles.	What is done in writing must be accurate and valid.
Methodically organized decision making.	Impulsive, spontaneous decision making.	Step-by-step approach to decision making.
Profit motive or good of individual ultimate aim.	What is good for group is good for the individual.	Good of group is the ultimate aim.
Decision making impersonal. Avoid involvement or conflict of interest.	Personalism necessary for good decision making.	Cultivate good emotional social setting for decision making; get to know decision maker.

[20] Pierre Casse, *Training for the Multinational Manager*, Society for Intercultural Training and Research.

Negative Messages

There are important distinctions in the way different cultures view negative messages: saying "no," for example, or passing bad news. In some cultures, you cannot assume that "yes" means agreement or understanding. Nor can you assume that "maybe" means maybe. Indirection is often used in order to avoid rudeness. In China, "perhaps," "maybe," and "We'll consider it" are polite ways of saying "no." When something is "inconvenient," it is most likely downright impossible. "Maybe it is time to go" means "It **is** time to go."

The visiting American representative of a major insurance company invited a number of Koreans to an official party celebrating a business deal. Half said "yes." Half said "maybe" or "perhaps." The caterer planned for a full house only to find that those who said "maybe" really meant "no."

There are cultures in Asia where saying "no" is a breach of manners. A "yes, but..." reveals resistance. When negotiations are not going well and no agreement is at hand, those cultures that abhor conflict may retreat. This does not necessarily mean a rejection of the negotiations, but an uninformed Westerner might well interpret it as such.

The solution, of course, is to educate yourself on the attitudes that your host country or foreign visitor holds regarding "negative" messages and rudeness. Don't let misunderstanding subvert a potentially fruitful relationship.

Emotion and Silence

Forms of emotional expression vary greatly around the world. The kiss, for example, is not universally associated with love or romance. Some see kissing as unsanitary and crude, particularly public kissing. For some, men and women shouldn't even touch in public.

Some Far Eastern cultures see Americans as impulsive and emotional. Latin Americans, however, see us as cold and controlled *hombres de hielo* (men of ice). Europeans find us noisy and brash, while we stereotype the British as aloof and the French as condescending. In the Arab world, men weep freely.

An American working for an elevator company spoke of her experience in Russia as traumatic. "They thought we were tricky. They were rude, confrontational and loud. They wept openly at one meeting, yelled and said we were stupid." While this may have been an isolated event, there is the possibility that Russians do not differentiate between public and private emotional displays in the same way we do.

EXERCISE **36** **Choose one of the situations below and follow the instructions carefully.**

1. Choose a partner and an observer. With this team, invent a negotiation scenario. You should be from two different countries or cultures. Then carry on a dialogue for five minutes, trying to establish a relationship. Remember to listen and give face.

   The observer will comment on the discussion, and your peers will grade you on your application of the nine principles you've learned in this chapter. Be sure to tell us who you are and what you're negotiating.

2. Choose a partner and set up a negotiation between yourself and a foreign executive. Choose the country carefully. Try to pair up with someone from a culture or country different from your own. Again, follow the nine principles in this chapter, and then write up the results of your negotiation according to the guidelines below:

Checklist for Contract Drafting[21]

Terms of contracts will vary depending on whether the agreement is a sales contract, technology transfer, joint venture or other transaction. A few considerations include:

1. State simply the intentions and purposes of both parties.
2. Describe the responsibilities of each party.
3. Define measures of accomplishment (how you'll determine that the job has been done) and methods for evaluation.
4. Agree on what standard principles of accounting will be used.

[21] Lennie Copeland and Lewis Griggs, *Going International* (New York, 1985).

5. Make provisions (as applicable) for:

- delivery and terms
- payment and credit
- security
- dispute resolution
- taxes (local and foreign)
- controlling language
- licenses
- expenses of personnel
- guarantees and insurance
- safeguarding of trade secrets
- installation and start-up costs
- quality control
- disclosure of information
- duties and other charges
- penalties and sublicensing rights
- work permits and entry visas.

24

P R I N C I P L E

Master Electronic Communication

The electronic global village is already a reality.

Bill Gates

The last decade has seen a revolution in office technology. Computers, voice mail, E-Mail, fax machines and other electronic innovations have become an indispensable part of doing business. While communication technology has brought speed and flexibility to the workplace, it has also brought confusion:

- What are the guidelines for effective voice mail?
- What are the guidelines for effective E-Mail?
- What is an electronic bulletin board?

Just as in traditional office communications, there are guidelines for the new technology. The basic principles are the same: clarity, brevity and precision. But the application of these principles varies depending on the type of communication you use.

Voice Mail

Voice mail has all but replaced the answering machine in many offices. It is an automated answering system capable of flexible responses based on the caller's use of telephone buttons. A complex system may filter the caller down through many choices to help direct his or her call to the correct party.

One of the clear advantages of voice mail is its ability to avoid "telephone tag." We've all experienced the frustrating back-and-forth attempt to connect with someone by phone, often just to get a quick "yes" or "no" to a simple question. Voice mail (and E-Mail) can expedite this kind of communication by eliminating delays and missed messages.

Voice mail can be a convenient tool, but any tool can be abused. The very ease of leaving voice mail can invite long-winded, rambling messages that waste the listener's time. When leaving voice mail, try to follow these simple rules:

1. Leave your **name** (and your company's name if appropriate)

2. Give the **time** of your call (and the date if appropriate)
   Don't say "I need an answer within the hour" or "...by this afternoon" if the receiver won't know the time or day of your call.

3. State the purpose of your call **clearly and briefly**
   Don't ramble. You should know precisely what you're going to say before you pick up the phone.

4. Leave your phone number **slowly** (or repeat it)
   Most of us can rattle off our number rapidly, but remember the person at the other end has to write down a string of unfamiliar numbers.

E-Mail

Electronic Mail (E-Mail) is fast replacing the traditional memo in many large businesses. E-Mail allows the sender to type a message on a computer terminal and instantly send it to one or more recipients. The recipient checks an electronic "in-box" on a terminal and reads the message. E-Mail, like voice mail, allows the sender to control when the message is sent and the receiver to control when the message is received. Unlike voice mail, E-Mail systems allow the sender to compose and edit the message for clarity. E-Mail systems also keep a complete record of all correspondence in the computer's storage areas.

E-Mail has revolutionized communications in the office. However, the ease of creating and forwarding messages frequently inundates users with messages. Many active correspondents report receiving over 100 messages a day. Computer science is currently exploring ways to winnow out electronic "junk mail" using artificial intelligence.

Although E-Mail allows fast and efficient delivery of messages, E-Mail's technology does not guarantee that the receiver will understand the message. E-Mail is different from paper communications, and techniques that might lead to an effective memo sometimes get in the way of an effective E-Mail message.

All standard commercial E-Mail messages consist of two parts: the address and the body (commonly called a "message"). Many systems allow "attachments" to an E-Mail message. These are simply electronic files that the sender transmits along with the message.

There are certain characteristics to E-Mail that have no paper analogue: Messages are forwardable. E-Mail systems allow the recipient to resend a received message to others. A message may be distributed and redistributed. Users are frequently surprised at how far their original messages travel. People who are complete strangers to the recipient may see the message appear on their screen.

If the message contains private information, explicitly request that the recipient not forward the message.

In most cases, it is better not to use E-Mail for messages that contain sensitive information.

E-Mail messages in a company-owned system are **not** private. In a company-owned E-Mail system, management has a right to examine the contents of any and all messages. Most companies restrict the use of E-Mail to company business and consider any other messages a misuse of company property. The Electronic Communications Privacy Act of 1986, the only federal law to govern E-Mail, protects users of public systems but explicitly exempts private systems. (The first amendment, in general, does not apply to internal business communications. Your company can — and probably does — limit the types of messages sent on their systems.)

The "Ollie North" rule: Colonel Oliver North, of Iran-Contra fame, was a heavy user of the White House E-Mail system. Although all messages within the system were deleted by both the sender and receiver, both the special prosecutor and the Tower Commission were able to subpoena the backup tapes that were routinely made by the computer systems personnel and reconstruct his messages.

Never use E-Mail for secret messages.

Make no assumption that deleted messages are non-retrievable.

Careful use of grammar and punctuation is essential. Although the intended recipient may be forgiving of errors, he or she may forward the message to others who may be less than impressed. Because face-to-face communication and even telephone communication is fast being replaced by E-Mail, senders should be just as concerned with message appearance as they would in a more personal encounter. A poorly spelled, ungrammatical message is the electronic equivalent of sloppy dressing or bad manners.

A message should contain only one idea or question.

If a message contains more than one idea, the recipient is often at a loss as to how to reply.

It forces the recipient to construct elaborate replies that are difficult to match with the original message. In many systems, it is difficult for a recipient to scroll through a complex message while creating a reply on-screen, which frequently means that the recipient might only respond to a few points instead of all points in a memo. Many E-Mail systems allow the user to store messages for later retrieval. If a message contains many ideas, it confounds most filing organizations so that the user will have difficulty retrieving the message.

To: Mike Feldman
From: Constance Confusion
Subject: Many things

1. Should I go on the business trip to Europe?
2. Did you receive my report on lack of parking spaces at the Home Office?
3. Should I take a course on Business Writing?

> The example above is poor. It is difficult to reply without repeating each point in the memo, and it will be impossible to find the memo later because of its indistinct subject.

State the subject of the message clearly and concisely.

> Recipients often have to sort through many incoming messages and should not be forced to read the message to decide its priority.

Use correct capitalization for a more professional look.

> An "ALL CAPS" message shouts to the recipient.

To: Mike Feldman
From: Harry Harangue
Subject: MEETING

PLEASE MEET ME FOR LUNCH TOMORROW. I HEAR THE NEW DELI IS EXCELLENT AND I WANT TO TRY THEIR PASTRAMI. BRING THE DAVIS ACCOUNT SO WE CAN GO OVER IT BEFORE THE AFTERNOON MEETING.

A lowercase message looks lazy.

To: Mike Feldman
From: Cathy Caplock
Subject: new strategy

your new strategy on new york sales report impressed me. i will take it up with the chairman of the board and let you know how he reacts. i hope there won't be a problem with sam's last report; it was pretty confusing to everyone at the meeting.

Messages should not exceed one screen.

The recipient should be able to view the entire message without scrolling the screen. Many systems, because of response time and performance constraints, perform at a much slower rate than word processors. Therefore, looking at more than a screenful of information is time consuming. A busy executive, faced with dozens of messages, will rarely look beyond the first page. If a message is not succinct enough to fit on one screen, either paper documents or electronic attachments should be used.

Bulletin Boards

Electronic bulletin boards, like E-Mail systems, contain messages. However, like a real bulletin board, the messages are posted publicly. Bulletin boards are used as forums to make inquiries, promote discussions or provide information. Thousands of bulletin boards have sprung up throughout the world providing electronic forums covering every conceivable subject. Even on commercial bulletin board systems, such as Prodigy or Compuserve, topics range from alternative life styles to model airplane building.

Bulletin board users have developed their own cryptic dialects. For example, "to flame" means to become mad at something. The symbol :-) means "smile." (Hint: look at the symbol sideways.)

Bulletin board messages often provoke "chains" of messages — where a user tacks one message onto another message electronically.

This is a typical message chain:

Gary,

re <<Using the term "ReaganBush" is akin to saying "ApplesOranges". >> Are you comparing the last 12 years with fruit salad? :-) See the following message thread for some additional opinions.

Ron,

Yes, you're right, more than 57% voted against Bush, ditto Perot. My point was that Clinton was *not* an overwhelming favorite. He was a lukewarm choice.

It's not what I'd call a landslide. Besides, we don't have Bush or Perot telling us to "contribute," now, do we?

Bob,

Perot may not have used the word "contribute" but he sure did call for increased taxes on those best able to pay. Combine his vote with Clinton's on those economic issues, and Bush was humiliated.

Ron,

At least Perot was honest enough to use the word "sacrifice," as in "involuntary but necessary." "Contribute" (to rehash an old subject) insults my intelligence. If you're going to steal my money, don't try to convince me that I'm making a voluntary donation.

Electronic forums, such as bulletin boards, are revolutionizing communications. People who are normally shy become outspoken; people who are geographically dispersed become close friends; people who are house-bound become active participants in discussions. There are many reports of marriages between electronic correspondents. All that is needed is an inexpensive computer, a phone line, and a modem (the device that connects the computer to the phone line).

Information Services

There are a number of on-line databases that provide access to business news, stock quotations and other current information. You can access this data from a computer/modem combination, much as you would call a bulletin board. Some of the most useful databases are:

- ABI/Inform – Lists article abstracts from business journals
- Dow Jones News Retrieval – Lists useful business and financial information
- Dun & Bradstreet – Lists useful information on over one million companies
- Electronic Yellow Pages – Lists names, addresses, etc. of 10 million US businesses
- Standard & Poor's News – Lists up-to-the-minute financial news

Hypertext

As electronic communication matures, authors will explicitly create documents for onscreen viewing. Both electronic mail messages and bulletin board messages resemble paper notes. However, the computer offers other, more powerful, mechanisms. Researchers are now exploring a technique called hypertext that promises to extend the potential of the paper document by using the power of a computer.

In a typical hypertext system, an author creates small, screen-size "chunks" of information. These chunks may consist of paragraphs of text, pictures or even audio or video fragments. The author then electronically connects these chunks with "links."

In a simple example, an author of a business writing text might construct the following paragraph:

What makes a written document credible? A written document or speech must have that quality Aristotle called **ethos** to be accepted as true and trustworthy.

230

If the reader did not know the word "ethos," he or she would use the computer's mouse to click on that word. When that happened, a box would appear with a definition:

Figure 24-1

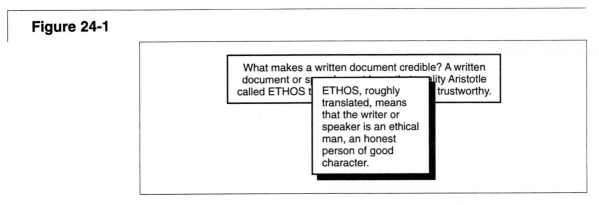

This is an example of a "vocabulary link." The author is spared from defining words within the text and a knowledgeable reader is spared having to read a definition. There are several characteristics of hypertext:

The text is not sequential. In the above example, the user can choose to follow the link or to ignore it. In many systems, the base text (the text first seen by the reader) is simply an outline. The reader then clicks on areas of interest. At that point, more outlines or summaries appear. More clicking gets the user deeper and deeper into the detail of the subject.

Text is non-redundant. Many traditional authors are forced to repeat details in different sections of a text for clarity. With hypertext, only a link is needed to refer to previous sections.

Multi-media texts are possible. For example, in a book about oral presentations, the user could click on a link and hear Martin Luther King, Jr., give his famous "I Have a Dream" speech. More sophisticated systems could even show a video clip of the same speech on the computer screen.

Educators are the primary users of hypertext. Text books are ideal for electronic translation and computers are widely available in an academic setting. The ease of zooming from a macro level to the most microscopic details, along with the potential for multimedia, greatly enhances the ability of students to learn from the hypertext.

C O N C L U S I O N

Parting Words

Writing is endlessly perfectible. No one can say, "I've arrived. I'm the best writer I can be." There will always be challenges to stretch you. Having mastered the principles in this book, you will begin to think about audience, layout, clarity...

But now you're going in the right direction. Since you'll have to write every day, why not make business writing an art, not a dull, life-sapping task? Even more likely, you will be dealing with what others write. You can influence them without destroying their self-esteem by making suggestions based on the 24 principles you've learned here.

You will be far ahead of others who produce mediocre documents and who live in fear of having their inadequacies exposed. Now you can be confident. You know that you know. The rest is practice.

APPENDIX

The Gunning Fog Index

Heavy writing fogs up ideas. This formula measures how much fog a given document contains.

1. Figure the average number of words per sentence in the sample passage. In other words, count the total number of words and divide by the number of sentences.

2. Figure the percentage of "hard" words (polysyllables) in the passage. That is, count the number of polysyllables and divide by the total number of words. Count as a polysyllable any word of three or more syllables, with these three exceptions:

   - **Proper Nouns**: that is, the capitalized names of people, places, companies, and products. Count them as "easy" words no matter how large they are.

   - **Combination Words**: large words made up of whole smaller words, such as "horsepower" or "another" or "nevertheless."

   - **Certain Verbs**: those which become three syllables by the addition of endings such as "-ed", "-es", or "-ing." For example, "sentences" or "including."

3. In step 1, you counted the average number of words per sentence in the passage. In step 2, you counted the number of polysyllables in the passage. Now add the results of steps 1 and 2 and multiply by .4 to determine the Fog Index.

4. **What should the Fog Index be?** For readable writing, the ideal Fog Index is between 10 and 12. Anything between 8 and 14 is acceptable. Over 14, the writing is unnecessarily heavy and bloated. Under 8, the writing may be overly simplistic and monotonous.

For example, this page and the previous one (including this last paragraph) have a Fog Index of 9.80. There are 311 total words (including numbers), divided by 24 sentences, giving an average of 12.9 words per sentence. There are 36 polysyllables, divided by 311 total words, giving an 11.6% ratio. Adding these two numbers and multiplying by .4 gives: 12.9 plus 11.6 times .4 equals 9.80, a very readable index.

A P P E N D I X

A Few Grammar and Punctuation Rules

1. **That / Which Clauses:** "That" and "Which" are **not** interchangeable.

   That clauses introduce essential information about a thing.
   Which clauses introduce incidental information about a thing.

   That clauses are not accompanied by commas.
   Which clauses are accompanied by commas.

   The Apple computer that I bought last week is broken.

   The phrase *that I bought last week* defines exactly which Apple computer (out of an unknown number) I am referring to.

   The Apple computer, which I bought last week, is broken.

   The phrase *which I bought last week* is an aside. It says "Oh, by the way, I bought that broken computer last week."

Compare:

The book that I wrote is on the table.
The book, which I wrote, is on the table.

The first sentence defines the book as the one I wrote, while the second just mentions in passing that I'm the author.

Which refers to things.
That refers to either things or an animal without a name.
Who is only for people or animals without names.

Examples:

a. Here comes the man _____ killed the rat _____ swallowed the cat.
b. He is the rat _____ lives on my block.
c. The rat sat in the hat _____ was empty.
d. Employees _____ plan to apply should fill out the application fully.
e. There is a matter about _____ more information is needed.
f. The number of unnecessary reports _____ are on my desk is shocking.

2. **Who & Whom**

The use of **who** and **whom** in questions is no longer reducible to a strict law. In modern spoken English **whom** is going out of use: **"Who** do you know?" In subordinate clauses the following rule still applies:

Who is used as the subject of a sentence or a clause.
Whom is the direct object of a verb or preposition.

Examples:

a. Pete is the man _____ discovered the rat.
b. This is the man _____ I met looking for the rat.
c. He is someone _____ is known for his rat extermination record.
d. The man _____ employs me allows me to say _____ is responsible.
e. The rat with _____ he was plotting the theft was a well-known broker.

3. **Sentence Logic:** There are four basic sentence constructions in English.

> **Simple:** *The cat ate the rat.*
> **Compound:** *The cat ate the rat, and the rat died.*
> **Complex:** *Although the cat ate the rat, the rat survived.*
> **Compound-complex:** *Although the cat ate the rat, the rat survived and the cat died.*

Write a simple sentence. Then write a compound, complex, and compound-complex sentence using the following conjunctions:

although	either/or
consequently	or
and	then
thus	moreover
otherwise	however
furthermore	therefore
yet	nevertheless

4. **Dangling Modifiers:** Avoid them.

> *The rat was caught using the trap.*
> *I enjoy watching the cat struggling to catch the rat from my study.*

Fix the following sentences to make them less ambiguous.

a. When using the proper apparatus the rat can be caught easily.
b. After finishing our reports they were sent to headquarters.
c. We only pay eligible benefits.

5. **Adverbs & Adjectives**

Distinguish between adverbs and adjectives:
Adverbs tell you about verbs (how something happens).
Adjectives describe nouns.

Examples:

a. You did that job (good, bad, well, badly).
b. Answer this question (quick, quickly).
c. Where is that (louse, lousy) rat staying?
d. He is such a (sweet, disgusting, perfect, wistfully) killer of rats.

6. **For Example / In Other Words:** The abbreviations *i.e.* and *e.g.* are **not** interchangeable.

   i.e. stands for the Latin phrase *id est* (it is) and means "in other words."
   e.g. stands for *exempli gratia* and means in Latin and English "for example."

   > *The current President (i.e., Bill Clinton) is a Democrat. Many recent Presidents (e.g., Nixon, Reagan, Bush) have been Republican.*

   i.e. and *e.g.* should be used within parentheses and punctuated as above. You can also simply write "for example" or "in other words."

7. **The Apostrophe**

   a. Use the apostrophe in contractions.

   > *isn't*
   > *couldn't*
   > *you're*

   b. Use the apostrophe to indicate possession.

   > *Lane's girlfriend*
   > *a stone's throw*
   > *two years' warranty*
   > *Johnny's house*
   > *the Jones's house*

   c. Use the apostrophe in plurals of lower case, and abbreviations.

   > *c's*
   > *CPA's*
   > *Ph.D's*

8. **The Comma**

   a. Use commas to set off introductory subordinate clauses, participial phrases, infinitive phrases, etc.

   > *If the cat eats the rat, the rat will die.*
   > *Having eaten the rat, the cat smiled.*
   > *To eat the rat, the cat had to catch him first.*
   > *Incidentally, the cat has eaten other rats.*

b. Use commas to set off words, phrases, and clauses in a series.

Open your mouth, swallow your mouse, and quit complaining!
The cat ate rats, mice and other tasty treats.

c. Use commas to separate coordinate clauses joined by **and**, **but**, **for**, **or**, **not**, and **yet**.

To be good is noble, but to eat rats is divine.

d. Use commas to set off nonrestrictive clauses.

My cat, who loves to lie in the sun, eats rats whenever possible.
The rat, who avoids sunny spots, isn't happy being a menu item.

e. Use commas to set off contrasting expressions.

The cat is getting fatter, not thinner.

9. **The Semicolon**

Use between main clauses that are not joined by one of the coordinate conjunctions (and, but, for, or, nor, yet, etc.).

The cat ate the rat; the rat survived.

Using a comma in this sentence is a serious error.

10. **The Colon**

a. Use to introduce a series of items.
b. Use to introduce long quotations or descriptions.
c. Use after words such as "the following" or "as follows."

11. **The Dash**

Use to indicate an abrupt break in thought. Do not use it in place of a comma, and be sure that the sentence would make sense if the portion within dashes were left out:

He was prepared to make any sacrifice — for a price.
He was prepared — for a price — to make any sacrifice.

Don't use dashes or bullets just for the sake of using them. Too many dashes make your page "busy." Bullets should be used to draw attention to important items, not to separate all the items neatly. Use indentation, white space, numbers, letters, bolding, etc.

12. **Parentheses**

Use to indicate a smoother break in thought than a dash. A parenthesis shouldn't affect the punctuation of the rest of the sentence (except in rare cases). When the parentheses are closed, continue the sentence as you would have normally:

The new software (DOS 5.0) will be delivered tomorrow.
We have purchased new software (DOS 5.0), and it will arrive tomorrow.
Tomorrow we will get the new software (DOS 5.0).

If you need to punctuate within parentheses, punctuate the rest of the sentence normally:

His new car (a Rolls-Royce!) will arrive tomorrow.
He bought a new car (a Rolls-Royce!), and it's arriving tomorrow.
He just bought a new car (a Rolls-Royce!).

Avoid overusing parentheses. *Send me thirty (30) copies* is redundant.

13. **Quotation Marks**

Punctuation within quotes is complicated. Remember these rules:

- Commas and periods always go **inside** the closing quote.
- Colons and semicolons always go **outside** the closing quote.
- Question marks and exclamation marks can go **inside or outside** depending on what they are punctuating.

He said, "Call me next week."
"Call me next week," he said.

He said, "Call me next week"; and I said, "O.K."
"Call me next week": that's what he said.

"Should I call him next week?" I wondered.
Should I have said, "Call me next week"?

14. **The Hyphen**

    a. Use to form a compound expression used as a single modifier.
    Is this cat a rat-eater?

    b. Use in compound words in which the hyphen is part of the accepted spelling.
    My cat is a master of rat-control.

    c. Use to divide words (between syllables) at the end of a line.

15. **Capitalization**

    <u>Capitalize</u>
    I'm taking Cost Accounting II.
    I'm taking courses in French and English.
    President Smith is here.
    I live on the West Coast.
    Mother is pretty.
    The Mississippi River is deep.
    He said, "We shall win."

    <u>Don't Capitalize</u>
    I'm majoring in accounting.
    I'm taking courses in history and math.
    The president of the company is here.
    I live out west.
    My mother is pretty.
    The river is deep.
    He said that we shall win.

APPENDIX

Using Numbers

1. <u>Generally</u>, spell out numbers under ten. Use figures for numbers over ten.

   We have been in operation for eight years.
   This is our 25th year of operation.

   BUT:

2. Never start a sentence with a figure.

   Right: *Fifty dollars is the admission charge.*
   Wrong: *50 dollars is the admission charge.*

3. Be consistent in expressing numbers in a series. If you begin with figures, stick with figures. If you begin with words, stick with words.

   He had three sales over seventeen days.
   We ordered 18 computers, 7 printers, and 3 modems.
   They were absent for 14 hours, 3 minutes.

4. Always use figures for ages.

   He is 6 years old, but his sister is 17.

5. Use figures for measurements.

   He is 6 feet 11 inches tall.
   OR *The screen is 3'10".*

6. Use figures for dates.

   He retired on June 5, 1993.
   His grandmother told him about the Roaring 20s.

7. Use figures for money.

   The firm lost $200,000 last year.
   John owes me $3.75.
   Lend me 50 cents.

8. Spell out amounts over $1 million.

   Ross Perot is worth $10 billion.
   John won $2.5 million in the lottery.

9. When quoting foreign currency amounts, show dollar amounts also.

   The expense account was £27 ($43.50) per diem for meals.
   It's not unusual to spend ¥1,650 ($15) for a hamburger in Tokyo.

10. Use figures and decimals for percentages.

    Right: *He earned a 6 percent raise.*
    Wrong: *He earned a six percent raise.*
    Right: *He earned a 6.25 percent raise.*
    Wrong: *He earned a 6¼ percent raise.*

11. Use figures with time of day (except with o'clock).

    Meet me in my office at 4 p.m.
    Meet me in my office at four o'clock.

APPENDIX

Deductive Syllogisms[22]

The traditional way of expressing a logical argument is in a syllogism. A syllogism is a kind of verbal mathematics: $a + b = c$ (or $1 + 2 = 3$). It is composed of three statements: the major premise, the minor premise, and the conclusion. Here is an example:

> All bachelors are unmarried.
> John is a bachelor.
> Therefore, John is unmarried.

The major premise is the first statement. It is called major because it contains the *major term* of the syllogism (in this case *unmarried*). The major term always appears as the predicate of the conclusion. The *minor term* (in this case *John*) always appears as the subject of the conclusion. The *middle term* (bachelor) does not appear in the conclusion, but is the common element, the connector between the premises.

---

[22] Adapted from *The Art of Thinking* by Vincent Ruggerio (New York, 1988), p. 212.

For analytic ease, and to help focus on structure instead of content, logicians often substitute symbols for the terms in a syllogism. The symbols most often used are P, Q and R. The syllogism above would be expressed symbolically as follows:

All P are Q.

R is P.

Therefore, R is Q.

Common Errors in Syllogisms

Before we turn to specific errors, it is necessary to clarify the concept of *distribution*. Distribution means making an assertion about *every* member of a class. Thus, in the statement "All colleges offer degrees," the subject is distributed. However, in the sentence "Some colleges offer degrees," the subject is undistributed.

There are four errors that frequently occur in syllogisms, and two related errors that, while not technically syllogistic, are similar in form. These errors are:

- Undistributed middle
- Illicit process
- Affirming the consequent
- Denying the antecedent
- Converting a conditional
- Negating antecedent and consequent.

Undistributed middle

Each middle term in a syllogism must be distributed at least once. If it is not distributed in either of the premises that it is intended to connect, then the reasoning is invalid.

Symbolic Expression	Example
All P are Q.	All wombats are fuzzy.
All R are Q.	All hedgehogs are fuzzy.
Therefore, all P are R.	Therefore, all wombats are hedgehogs.

Illicit process

Any term in a syllogism that is distributed in the conclusion must also be distributed in the premise in which it occurs. If either the major or minor term is distributed in the conclusion but not in the premise in which it occurs, the syllogism is invalid.

<u>Symbolic Expression</u> Illicit Major	<u>Example</u>
All P are Q. No R are P. Therefore, no R are Q.	All wombats are animals. No sheep are wombats. Therefore, no sheep are animals.

<u>Symbolic Expression</u> Illicit Minor	<u>Example</u>
All P are Q. Some R are P. Therefore, all R are Q.	All bachelors are unmarried. Some politicians are bachelors. Therefore, all politicians are unmarried.

The four remaining errors occur in hypothetical (if-then) reasoning. They are all corruptions of the following *legitimate* form of hypothetical reasoning:

<u>Symbolic Expression</u>	<u>Example</u>
If P, then Q. P. Therefore, Q.	If I eat dorm food, I will get sick. I ate dorm food. Therefore, I will get sick.

Affirming the consequent

<u>Symbolic Expression</u>	<u>Example</u>
If P, then Q. Q. Therefore, P.	If I eat dorm food, I will get sick. I am sick. Therefore, I ate dorm food.

Denying the antecedent

<u>Symbolic Expression</u>	<u>Example</u>
If P, then Q. Not P. Therefore, not Q.	If I eat dorm food, I will get sick. I did not eat dorm food. Therefore, I will not get sick.

Converting a conditional

Symbolic Expression	Example
If P, then Q.	If I get a headache, I take aspirin.
Therefore, if Q, then P.	Therefore, if I take aspirin, I get a headache.

Negating antecedent and consequent

Symbolic Expression	Example
If P, then Q.	If you take my advice, you will get rich.
Therefore, if not P, then not Q.	Therefore, if you don't take my advice, you won't get rich.

A P P E N D I X

Answers to Exercises

Exercise 1

Even though unemployment has been low, we can't keep up with our workload. Time-lapse comparisons show that we

- cannot respond to floods of appeals from employers
- cannot handle the monthly deluge of referee decisions
- cannot meet holiday time off
- cannot cope with the slightest absenteeism
- cannot set aside a minute for training.

We need help.

We need it in any classification — supervisors, fact finders, claims examiners and clerks.

A solution: We could share a technician, a fact finder, a claim examiner, and a typist for 2–3 days a week with another unit. Obviously, the units would have to work out schedules so that each unit would know what staff to count on each day; and only fully competent staff should be assigned to this shared work.

Exercise 2

1. The tone is impersonal, intimidating, and robot-like. Try to sound more human.
2. Too wordy. "For safety, use gloves and wash your hands" is the essence of the message.
3. This is, in every sense of the term, "unspeakable" prose.
4. This is also too verbose. You would never speak this.
5. Awkward and wordy.
6. Far too wordy. The Plain English Dictionary would help here.
7. These openings are too stiff and formal. You would never speak this way.
8. Very impersonal. Too much passive voice.

Exercise 3

1. Both are fine, but the second is a bit less formal and the emphasis is different.
2. Again, both are fine, but contractions make the style more informal.
3. That is something in which the CEO is interested.

    • OK, but *very* formal.

That is something the CEO's interested in.
That's something the CEO's interested in.

    • It is a **false rule** that you should never end a sentence with a preposition (see H.W. Fowler's *Dictionary of Modern English Usage*). Winston Churchill, when criticized for ending sentences with prepositions, said, "That is a piece of errant pedantry up with which I will not put."

The CEO is interested in that product.

    • This is the best choice.

4. The first sentence is too wordy. The second and third are both pompous and abstract. The fourth is the best.
5. Far too formal. You wouldn't speak "of which many."
6. Too wordy and impersonal.
7. The phrase "distributed herewith" is unnecessary legalese. "And/or" is ambiguous.

Exercise 4

1. The participants discussed the future of the program for several months to determine its validity.
2. Here is a summarized report. The details are in a separate volume.

Exercise 5

You don't need to avoid the left column **always**. Just don't **overuse** it.

Exercise 6

1. Your April 28, 1988, orientation was informative and very well presented. I would like to participate in any future programs of this kind.
2. On April 20, 1987, the District Court of Springfield issued an Execution for $1,342.70 (see our April 15 letter for more details).
3. The University of Connecticut is responsible for **all** invoices that are:
   a. covered by valid proofs of delivery
   b. accepted by a university representative.

4. I don't know.
5. If the job interests you, this could be a good career move.
6. We indicated in our September meeting that we needed to give more thought to the future roles of women in our department.
7. We need to study the structure of the organization in order to determine (a) the best control system, and (b) the best rating system.

Exercise 7

1a. Households with small children (where mothers work or fathers are absent) need community-supported day care. Families with a higher income level can more easily afford good private care. Census reports can give valuable information such as:

- number of working mothers who:
  have children under six
  live with their husbands

- number of families that:
  have no father present
  have income below poverty line
- average number of children who:
  are under six
  live in such families.

This kind of information can be helpful when we need to know:
  how many mothers are interested in day care
  how many children are involved
  where the best location would be.

1b. Neighborhoods may need community-supported day care facilities for working mothers with small children. A census report can help evaluate the need for such facilities.

2. We worked hard to develop an effective certification plan for our four nuclear plant simulators. Our team designed the program to:

   1. provide for initial certification according to requirements of the Nuclear Regulatory Commission.

   2. ensure that we comply with the requirements of the Connecticut Health and Safety Board.

   In our plan, we focused on a formal Certification Program that includes simulator configuration management. We will have to commit ourselves to this management for the life of the simulator. The Certification concentrates on the following tasks:

   1. updating the design database

   2. implementing plant design changes

   3. resolving simulator deficiencies

   4. testing and documenting performance.

Exercise 8

The Budget Analyst assists the Budget Officer in all aspects of budget management for the Office of the Secretary and its independently administered agencies. Responsibilities include:

1. Consolidating information, requests, program evaluation, and analysis and review of the operations of the Secretariat.

2. Reviewing the relevance and cost-effectiveness of all programs submitted.
3. Assisting in the planning and development of reports for the Secretariat's independent agencies.
4. Participating in all aspects of funds control and analysis.

Exercise 9

1. The job responsibilities include:

   - Processing accurate and timely mortgage collection reports from assigned correspondents; processes and rejects weekly corrections to transactions.
   - Auditing monthly billings for accuracy of balances and installments with corrections noted before mailing.
   - Corresponding with office regarding discrepancies and resolving problems associated with accurate processing of reports or other related matters.

2. Our Property Insurance will:

   - cover on an "all risks" basis (versus named perils)
   - bring all local policies to a company standard
   - increase the current $50 million limit to $75 million on Dec. 1st
   - offer a $25,000 deductible, if there is no local coverage in place.

     EXAMPLE: If lightning damage isn't covered under your local policy, the master policy provides the coverage subject to a $25,000 deductible.

3. XYZ Corporation is the world's largest manufacturer of widgets, wadgets, and gizmos, with 1992 revenues $3.6 billion. Over 75% of these revenues came from foreign sales. Our global presence is a result of:

   - 50,000 employees worldwide.
   - 30 manufacturing facilities in 19 countries (with products sold in 163 of the world's 171 nations).
   - 1700 service locations worldwide.

Exercise 10

1. We were affected by (a) the uncertainty of their policy on outside contacts, and (b) the difficulty of their pursuing information from those contacts without causing problems for the company.

2. The project will collate existing approaches to:
   - strategic decision making in enterprise
   - public policy formation
   - program management.

   It will also evaluate:
   - practical approaches for developing countries
   - new approaches to further development.

3. A project of this type could support our work with:
   a. food and agriculture policy
   b. agricultural planning
   c. effectiveness analysis for other programs such as health and nutrition
   d. administrative reform.

4. Our personnel provide support to the educational system through (a) tutoring local students, (b) assisting teachers in business encounters, and (c) cooperating with local school systems and boards of education.

5. There is no doubt that we need to work on several weaknesses: free-throw percentage, shot selection, man-to-man defense.

6. Donna (Legal Assistant of our litigation team) is responsible for determining the accuracy and integrity of all the data loaded in the system, and assisting with the identification of current and future needs of the departments supported by the system.

Exercise 11

1. Remember that whenever a particular exposure warrants Loss Prevention services, you should visit the appropriate Loss Prevention worker to help contain the problem.

2. This pilot program will prepare banks to spur the economic development of neighborhoods, communities, and the region as a whole.

3. Preparing middle managers for more substantial tasks continues to challenge institutions.

Exercise 12

1. This may interest Stu as he analyzes the quotes.
2. The U.S. and the Soviet Union agree with the principles of German reunification.
3. After consulting with Sales, I've decided to reduce the inventory of ...
4. We will adjust the spring tension in ...
5. Please list all the purple and green imitation lizard watchbands with brass-plated buckles.
6. The improvement of market share reflects less absenteeism.
7. This year has been problematic.
8. The CEO stated to the Board that we mustn't have an increase in inventory backlogs.
9. We'll transfer assets today.
10. We've reviewed the roster file listing.
11. We spoke yesterday on the phone about ...
12. We have calculated the July monthly report.
13. After much investigation, we've decided to change our position.

Exercise 13

1. Could be a justifiable passive if it doesn't matter who did it.
2. We will replace...
3. The rate of progress amazed the OMB Directors.
4. Obvious attempt to lessen the agent's responsibility.
5. A programmable calculator will determine the intervals.
6. Justifiable passive.
7. Could be justifiable.

8. We'll attach a form to each policy so every transaction will have a separate endorsement.

9. Ginny provided the information.

10. Justifiable passive.

11. We studied all incoming bills of lading.

12. Who did it?

Exercise 14

1. We decided the study should include special files.

2. His sources were often dates.

3. We thought trips to New York would be infrequent.

4. Note: The team suggested this early in the process.

5. They marketed the product when they started the firm.

6. We will distribute all products by 1995.

7. Recommendation: Include a team in the final evaluation.

8. I feel the technical people need to raise their level of performance.

9. Voltage or reactive performance might change during the time allotted.

10. The group should include four to six regular members and an indefinite number of liaison members.

11. Group members will have a limited time commitment.

12. The company will distribute all the products.

Exercise 15

1. We encourage you to submit a bid for the new contract, following required bidding guidelines.

2. When our accounting office inflated the actual costs, we received many angry memos from within the company.

3. We would like you and your staff to attend the next sales meeting.

4. It would be wrong to conclude that all Savings and Loans are unsafe, and we should correct this false impression.

Exercise 16

Review résumés based on the examples in the book.

Exercise 17

Review letters based on the examples in the book.

Exercise 18

There is no set answer here. Judge the letters based on tone and attention to an appropriate audience.

Exercise 19

TO: Janet Peckinpaugh
FROM: Don Zimmer
SUBJECT: AIRPORT CONSTRUCTION IN GRENADA

The **purpose** of this memo is to:
- outline the information John Sanford, Congressional Research Services, requested.

The request was **on behalf of**:
- a Representative of the House; on the Foreign Relations Committee; a Democrat.

The request was **for**:
- info regarding AID's involvement in constructing Grenada's airport prior to 1979.

The **involvement** was:
- U.S., U.K. and Canada commissioned an economic survey of English-speaking Caribbean islands including Grenada (1966). **Recommendation:** Establish a regional development bank.
- UNDP team expanded the study (1967). **Recommendation:** Establish the Caribbean Development Bank (CDB).
- CDB was established (1970). Potential funding (by 1973) for Special Development Fund:

U.S.	$10 million
U.K.	$ 5 million
Canada	$ 5 million

- Grenada borrowed $50,400 from U.S., U.K. and Canada for an airport extension at Pearl (1972).
- AID loaned CDB $50,000 for airport construction at Carriacou (1973).
- U.S., U.K., Canada and the World Bank conducted a Feasibility Study for airport construction at Pearl (1976). **Recommendation:** Not cost effective. **Action:** None. Cubans offered to build a 9,000-foot runway at Point Salines.

Sources: AID, IMF. World Bank, Project Nos. 5380001, 5380003

Exercise 20
Employees with Performance Ratings Below "Fully Meets Expectations" and Performance Improvement Program.

CENTRAL REGION'S EMPLOYEES WHO FAIL TO MEET PERFORMANCE EXPECTATIONS.

Name	Rating	Reasons	Remarks
BILL	002	Attendance	Recovering from injury and light performance duty, but still not performing up to full extent of job classification.
			Absenteeism is a problem so he is on No-Work No-Pay status. Is not in a performance improvement program at this time.
Past Ratings:	002 2/1/89 002 7/16/88	003 7/6/87 002 7/6/86	
MARY	002	Performance	Does not consistently maintain "fully Meets expectations" status.
			Is in a performance improvement program.
Past Ratings:	003 consistently		
DAN	002	Attendance	Absenteeism is a result of war injuries and the nature of his work. He is very competent, however, when he is here.
			He is on No-Work No-Pay status, and his attendance is improving.
Past Ratings:	002 2/1/89 002 2/1/88		

Exercise 21
Review structures based on the examples in the book.

Exercise 22
Review summaries based on the examples in the book.

Exercise 23
Review reports based on the examples in the book.

Exercise 24
There is no set answer here. Judge the responses based on the strength of the arguments and analogies.

Exercise 25
1. A causal link. Basing future prediction on past occurrences.
2. No causal link.
3. No causal link. This is an example of the Hawthorne Experiment.

Exercise 26

I.	1. E	III.	1. R
	2. R		2. E
	3. R		3. E
			4. E
II.	1. C		5. R
	2. R		6. C
	3. E		7. C

IV. Some of these have a mixture of rationales. Real-world writing does not always fit into tidy categories.

1. 5 (Causal)
2. 6 (Sign) and 4 (Alternative Claims)
3. 1 (Inductive) and 3 (Parallel)
4. 2 (Inductive)
5. 7 (Analogy)
6. 3 (Parallel)
7. 6 (Sign)
8. 4 (Alternative Claims)

Exercise 27
There is no set answer here. Judge the responses based on the strength of the arguments.

Exercise 28

1. 5
2. 2
3. 2
4. 3
5. 7
6. 1
7. 1
8. 2
9. 6
10. 6
11. 5
12. 8
13. 4
14. 9

Exercise 29

1. 2
2. 4
3. 3
4. 3
5. 3
6. 1

1. 5
2. 3
3. 2
4. 3
5. 4

Exercise 30

Judge the **effectiveness** based on the strength of the argument.

1. Logical error is COVERT PERSUASION, an appeal to fear. Implies that if you don't buy Northern Insurance, you'll be sorry.

2. Logical error is EITHER/OR.

3. Logical error is UNKNOWABLE STATISTIC.

4. Logical error is COVERT PERSUASION. Here it is an appeal to fear that your child might fall behind because of you.

5. This is a more subtle one. Logical error is based on wordplay. What does "fast" mean in this context? This is probably a false analogy.

Exercise 31

There is no set answer here. Judge the responses based on persuasiveness.

Exercise 32

There is no set answer here. Judge the responses based on the strength of the arguments.

Exercise 33

There is no set answer here. Judge the responses based on creativity. A possible answer for #6 might begin as follows:

STATEMENT OF PURPOSE
The purpose of this plan is to secure private financing for The Drawing Room. This business will be located in the La Brea neighborhood of Los Angeles and will be structured as a limited partnership. There will be nine Limited Partners who will invest $3,000 each (total $27,000).

DESCRIPTION OF THE BUSINESS
The Drawing Room will provide shared studio facilities and live models for artists. The studio will serve professional artists, amateur artists, art students and art enthusiasts. It will be open from 8:30 a.m. to 10:00 p.m. seven days a week. There will be four twelve-week semesters that will coincide with the academic semesters of fall, spring and summer.

THE MARKET
Full enrollment will consist of 1,000 people per year. The client profile would be:

- 10% professional artists
- 15% amateur artists
- 25% art enthusiasts
- 50% art students

Prices will be significantly below the competition in order to attract initial clientele. We will advertise using classified ads in the *Los Angeles Times*, the *Advocate*, art journals, and through fliers at area colleges and art supply stores.

Exercise 34

1. There are several possible answers here. One is that the girl uses a squirt gun as a joke. Another is that the man has the hiccups, and the girl tries to scare them away but doesn't know the gun is loaded.

2. One possible answer: She "accidentally" drops the stone she chooses and then says, "We can tell what color I chose by seeing the color of the stone left in the bag."

3 – 12. There are no set answers here. Judge the responses based on creativity.

Exercise 35

1. Sue is the "new kid" and has to earn the respect of her colleagues. She can help herself by being courteous and businesslike.

2. The kiss would be a major mistake. This is not France.

3. The visitor is correct in returning the applause. He is complimenting the workers, not himself.

4. There is no breach of protocol here. The American shows a good understanding of Indian customs.

Exercise 36

There is no set answer here. Judge the responses based on sensitivity to the other culture.

B I B L I O G R A P H Y

Adams, James L. *Conceptual Blockbusting: A Guide to Better Ideas*. New York: W.W. Norton & Co. Inc., 1979.

Anderson, Paul V. *Technical Writing: A Reader-Centered Approach*. New York: Harcourt, Brace, Jovanovich, 1987.

Axtell, Roger E. *Gestures: The Do's and Taboos of Body Language Around the World*. New York: John Wiley & Sons, Inc., 1991.

Bell, Kathleen. *Developing Arguments*. Belmont, CA: Wadsworth Publishing Co., 1990.

Bettinghaus, Erwin P. *Persuasive Communication*. New York: Holt, Rinehart & Winston, 1973.

Blackstone, William. *Commentaries on the Laws of England*. New York: W.E. Dean, 1852.

Bucholsky, Steve & Thomas Roth. *Creating the High Performance Team*. New York: John Wiley & Sons, 1987.

Bueler, Lois. *What We Do When We Think: Analogies and Test Cases*. A paper delivered at the CCCC Conference in Chicago, March 1990.

Bull, P.E. *Posture and Gesture*. New York: Pergamon Press, 1987.

Casse, Pierre. *Training for the Multinational Manager*. Society for Intercultural Training and Research. Washington: SIETAR International, 1982.

Clair, Susanne. *International Communications*. University of Connecticut: unpublished paper for Managerial Communications, 1991.

Copeland, Lennie & Lewis Griggs. *Going International*. New York: Penguin Books, 1985.

Davis, Stanley. *Future Perfect*. New York: Addison-Wesley Publications, 1987.

De Bono, Edward. *The CoRT Thinking Skills Program*. New York: Pergamon Press, 1984.

——————. *Lateral Thinking: Creativity Step By Step*. New York: Harper and Row, 1970.

_____. *New Think*. New York: Avon Books, 1967.

_____. *Practical Thinking: PO, Beyond Yes and No*. London: Penguin Books, 1973.

_____. *Six Thinking Hats*. Boston: Little Brown, 1985.

_____. *Six Action Shoes*. New York: Harper Collins, 1991.

_____. *Opportunities*. London: Penguin Books, 1978.

_____. *Serious Creativity*. New York: Harper Collins, 1992.

Decker, Burt. *You've Got to Be Believed to Be Heard*. New York: St. Martin's Press, 1991.

Driskill, Linda. *Business and Managerial Communication*. New York: Harcourt, Brace, Jovanovich, 1992.

Dulek, Fielden & Hill. "International Communication: An Executive Primer," in *Business Horizons*. Jan. – Feb. 1991.

Ehrlich, Eugene & Gene Hawes. *Speak for Success*. New York: Bantam Books, 1984.

Fahnestock, Jeanne & Marie Secor. *A Rhetoric of Argument*. New York: Random House, 1982.

Ferraro, Gary P. *The Cultural Dimension of International Business*. Englewood Cliffs, NJ: Prentice Hall, 1990.

Firestein, R.L. *From Basics to Breakthroughs*. East Aurora, NY: United Educational Services, 1988.

Flower, Linda. *Problem-Solving: Strategies for Writing*. New York: Harcourt, Brace, Jovanovich, 1981.

Fortenbaugh, W.W. *Aristotle on Emotion*. New York: Barnes and Noble, 1975.

Fowler, H.W. *A Dictionary of Modern English Usage*. New York : Oxford University Press, 1987.

Glenn, Witmeyer & Stevenson. "Cultural Styles of Persuasion," in *International Journal of Intercultural Studies*, London: Pergamon Press, Ltd., 1984.

Griffin, T.J. & W.R. Daggatt. *The Global Negotiator*. New York: Harper Brothers, 1990.

Gruner, C.R. "An Experimental Study of Satire," in *Speech Monographs*, no. 32 (1965).

Hall, Edward T. *Hidden Differences: Doing Business with the Japanese*. Yarmouth, ME: Intercultural Press, Inc., 1987.

_____. *The Silent Language*. Yarmouth, ME: Intercultural Press, Inc., 1987.

Hall, Edward T. & Mildred Hall. *Understanding Cultural Differences*. Yarmouth, ME: Intercultural Press, Inc., 1989.

Hartmann, G. "A Field Experiment on the Comparative Effects of Emotional and Rational Political Leaflets in Determining Election Results," in *Journal of Abnormal Social Psychology*, no. 31 (1936).

Harty, Kevin J. *Strategies for Business and Technical Writing*. New York: Harcourt, Brace, Jovanovich, 1989.

Isaksen, S.G. & D.J. Treffinger. *Creative Problem-Solving: The Basic Course*. Buffalo, NY: Bearly Ltd., 1985.

Jacobus, Lee A. *Writing and Thinking.* New York: Macmillan, 1989.

Jain, Subhash C. *Unpublished paper.* University of Connecticut, 1989.

Karlins, Marvin & Herbert Abelson. *Persuasion: How Opinions and Attitudes Are Changed.* New York: Springer Publishing Co., 1970.

Kiesler, Charles, et. al. *Attitude Change: A Critical Analysis of Theoretical Approaches.* New York: John Wiley & Sons, 1969.

Klauser, Henriette Anne. *Writing on Both Sides of the Brain.* San Francisco: Harper and Row, 1987.

Kohls, Robert. *Survival Kit for Overseas Living.* Yarmouth, ME: Intercultural Press, Inc., 1984.

Lear, Jonathan. *Aristotle and Logical Theory.* New York: Cambridge University Press, 1980.

Levin, Gerald. *Writing and Logic.* New York: Harcourt, Brace, Jovanovich, 1982.

Lutz, William. *Doublespeak.* New York: Harper and Row, 1989.

Malraux, André. *La Condition Humaine.* Paris: Gallimard, 1969.

Maslow, Abraham. *The Farther Reaches of Human Nature.* New York: Viking Press, 1973.

May, Rollo. *The Courage to Create.* New York: Norton, 1976.

Mayfield, Morley S. *Thinking for Yourself.* Belmont, CA: Wadsworth Publishing Co., 1987.

McCrosky, James C. *Studies of the Effects of Evidence in Persuasive Communication.* East Lansing: Michigan State University Press, 1967.

Mellinkoff, David. *The Language of the Law.* Boston: Little Brown & Co., 1963.

Minsky, Marvin. *The Society of Mind.* New York: Simon & Schuster, 1985.

Nisbett, R. & L. Ross. *Human Inference: Strategies and Shortcomings of Social Judgement.* Englewood Cliffs: Prentice Hall, 1980.

Oches, Norman. "Cross-Cultural Presentations: How to Make Them More Effective," in *Sales and Marketing Management.* September 1989.

Osborn, Alex F. *Applied Imagination: Principles and Procedures of Creative Problem-Solving.* New York: Scribner, 1979.

Parkhurst, William. *The Eloquent Executive.* New York: Avon Books, 1988.

Parnes, Sidney. *The Magic of Your Mind.* Buffalo, NY: Creative Education Foundation, 1981.

Pascale, P.B. & A.G. Athos. *The Art of Japanese Management.* New York: Simon and Schuster, 1981.

Pearsall, Thomas E. & Donald H. Cunningham. *How to Write for the World of Work.* Chicago: Holt, Rinehart & Winston, 1990.

Peoples, David. *Presentations Plus.* New York: John Wiley & Sons, 1988.

Petty, Richard E. & John T. Cacioppo. *Attitudes and Persuasion: Classic and Contemporary Approaches.* Dubuque, Iowa: William C. Browns, 1981.

Plunkett, Lorne, & Guy Hale. *The Proactive Manager*. New York: John Wiley and Sons, 1982.

Price, Jonathan. *Put That in Writing*. New York: Penguin Books, 1984.

Ray, Michael & Rochelle Ryers. *Creativity in Business*. Garden City, NY: Doubleday, 1988.

Rodopi, N.V. *Aristotle's Deduction and Induction*. Amsterdam: W.N. Thompson, 1975.

Roloff, Michael & Gerald R. Miller. *Persuasion: New Directions in Theory and Research*. London: Sage Publishing Co., 1980.

Rosenfield, Lawrence W. *Aristotle and Information Theory*. The Hague: Mouton, 1971.

Ruggerio, Vincent Ryan. *The Art of Thinking: A Guide to Critical and Creative Thought*. New York: Harper and Row, 1988.

Ruggerio, Vincent & Joan Vespar. *Contemporary Business Communication*. New York: Harper Collins, 1993.

Russell, Bertrand. *A History of Western Philosophy*. New York: Simon and Schuster, 1945.

Salmon, Merrilee H. *Logic and Critical Thinking*. New York: Harcourt, Brace, Jovanovich, 1989.

Snowdon, Sondra. *The Global Edge: How Your Company Can Win in the International Marketplace*. New York: McGraw-Hill, 1990.

Spring, S. & G. Deutsch. *Left Brain, Right Brain*. San Francisco: W.H. Freeman, 1981.

Spurgeon, Sally De Witt. *The Power to Persuade*. New York: Prentice Hall, 1985.

Tobias, Sheila. *They're Not Dumb; They're Different*. Research Corporation of the Advancement of Science, 1990.

Toulmin, Stephen. *An Introduction to Reasoning*. New York: Macmillan, 1979.

_____. *The Uses of Argument*. Cambridge: Cambridge University Press, 1958.

Van Alstyne, Judith S. *Professional and Technical Writing Strategies*. Englewood Cliffs, NJ: Prentice Hall, 1990.

Webbink, Patricia. *The Power of the Eye*. New York: Springer Publishing Co., 1986.

Whale, John. *Put It in Writing*. London: J.M. Dent & Sons, Ltd., 1984.

Wycoff, Joyce. *Mindmapping*. New York: Berkley Books, 1991.

Zimbardo, Philip & Ebbe B. Ebbessen. *Influencing Attitudes and Changing Behavior*. Reading, MA: Addison-Wesley Publishing Co., 1970.